REVOLUTIONARIES
of the SOUL

Other Titles by Gary Lachman

REVOLUTIONARIES
of the SOUL

Reflections on Magicians, Philosophers, and Occultists

GARY LACHMAN

This publication has been generously supported by
The Kern Foundation

QUEST

BOOKS

Theosophical Publishing House
Wheaton, Illinois * Chennai, India

Quest Books
Theosophical Publishing House
PO Box 270
Wheaton, IL 60187-0270

www.questbooks.net

Cover image: Serg64/Shutterstock.com
Cover design by Kirsten Hansen Pott
Typesetting by Wordstop

Library of Congress Cataloging-in-Publication Data

Lachman, Gary.
Revolutionaries of the soul: reflections on magicians, philosophers, and
occultists / Gary Lachman.—First Quest Edition.
        pages   cm
Includes bibliographical references and index.
ISBN 978-0-8356-0926-5
Occultists—Biography.   I. Title.
BF1408.L33 2014
130.92'2—dc23
[B]   2014012128

4 3 2 1 * 14 15 16 17 18 19 20

Printed in the United States

To revolutionaries of the soul everywhere

Table of Contents

Acknowledgments

"Colin Wilson and Faculty X" was first published in *Quest,* Summer 1995.

"Discovering Swedenborg" was first published in *Fortean Times* 220, March 2007.

"Jan Potocki and the *Saragossa Manuscript*" was first published in *Fortean Times* 140, November 2000.

"Éliphas Lévi: The Professor of Transcendental Magic" was first published in *Fortean Times* 120, March 1999.

"The Alchemy of August Strindberg" was first published in *Fortean Times* 180, February 2004.

"The Inimitable Madame B." was first published in *EnlightenNext* 47, Fall/Winter 2011.

"Rudolf Steiner: The Dweller on the Threshold" was first published in *Fortean Times* 205, January 2006.

"Manly Palmer Hall: The Secret Teacher" was first published in *Fortean Times* 255, November 2009.

"Dion Fortune: Psychic Warrior" was first published in *Fortean Times* 287, May 2012.

"Aleister Crowley: The Beast Himself" was first published in *Fortean Times* 231, January 2008.

"Julius Evola: Mussolini's Mystic" was first published in *Fortean Times* 191, Special Issue 2004.

"Jung and the Occult" was first published in *Fortean Times* 264, July 2010.

"Ouspensky in London" was first published in *Quest,* Autumn 1998.

ACKNOWLEDGMENTS

"Jean Gebser: Leaping into the Unknown" was first published in *EnlightenNext,* Spring/Summer 2010.

"Owen Barfield and the Evolution of Consciousness" was first published in *Lapis* 3, 1996.

"The Strange Death of James Webb" was first published in *Fortean Times* 150, September 2001.

I'd like to thank the editors of *Quest, Lapis,* and *EnlightenNext* for their assistance in making this book possible. My special thanks goes to David Sutton, my editor at *Fortean Times,* for his generous and invaluable help and to Joscelyn Godwin for his needed suggestions. I am also indebted to Anja Flode Bjorlo for her inestimable contribution and to Richard Smoley for seeing the thing through. And once again I'd like to thank my sons, Maximilian and Joshua, and their mother, Ruth Jones, for their unfailing support.

Introduction

Looking for the Invisible

The idea of becoming a writer first came to me in my teens. It was expressed then in some rather bad poetry—luckily this has not survived—and it was not until many years later that I actually produced anything worth reading, or at least that an editor would accept for publication. "Perseverance furthers," the *I Ching* tells us, and at least in this context it was right. Today, looking back to the time when I was first being published—the early 1990s, when I was about to enter my forties—I am amazed to realize that I have been writing now for more than twenty years. I started out with book reviews and magazine articles and essays, taking any opportunities that presented themselves and, as most beginning writers do, eagerly building up a body of work in print, doing all I could to make up for lost time. Today, in my late fifties, I am just as busy as I was then, even more so, suffering the full-time writer's complaint of chronic workaholism and insufficient earnings; even during the busiest days of my career as a musician—by the mid-70s I had turned the poetry into songwriting and was successful with it for a time—I was never as busy as I am now. But between first seeing print and today, I have—if I may so immodestly inform the reader— added a few notches to my belt. Between 2001, when my first book, *Turn Off Your Mind*, appeared and the time of this writing (2014), I have produced sixteen books, with another due to be published this year, and I am about to start the research for another, practically as soon as I finish writing this introduction. I have also produced scores of articles, essays, book reviews, interviews, and lectures, of which the pieces collected here are a small sample. It often feels that I do very little other than write—a complaint friends often make—and that I have become, as a less-busy fellow writer once called me, a "writing machine." If that is the case, it is the one example of a man-machine merger that I condone, and I trust that the gods of writings—such as Hermes, about whom I have, ironically, written a book—will keep me well oiled and in good working order for at least another twenty years.

What often prevents an aspiring writer from really getting started is the problem of finding his material, his theme—what, exactly, to write about. (Creative writing teachers tell us to "write about what you know," but that only raises the question: what do you know?) The technical tricks of the trade, of course, have to be mastered and a readable style developed. But what leads to mastery is the key element of having something to say, of finding the things that you love and are obsessed with and that you want to introduce readers to, so as to stimulate an equal love and obsession in them. It is precisely that love and obsession that drives the writer to finding the best way to communicate his passion.

What the reader of this collection, and perhaps of my other books, will discover is that I am in love and obsessed with ideas. I like to think. It is, admittedly, an occupation not as popular as in some earlier times and one that requires the increasingly elusive necessities of peace and quiet, along with the more accessible ingredients of a book, notebook, table, and pen, or, more frequently today, laptop. You don't need a Hadron collider or Hubble telescope or Human Genome Project—just time, dedication, and an insatiable need to clarify and focus your mind. I am no critic of intuition, feeling, or the more palpable delights of sensation, but I do think that human beings are essentially *thinking* beings. That is to say, it is in the world of the mind that our humanity truly resides; it is the element that, as far as we know, we do not share with other creatures and which, for better or worse, it has been given to us to explore. This is why it is not as popular an activity as some others. Thinkers are rather like those people at the head of a jungle expedition, hacking into a thick tangle of roots and vines in order to make a path. It is demanding, unpleasant work, but it needs to be done, and it must be admitted that the people further back on the trail have a relatively easier time of it. Is it any surprise that most of them leave the difficult work to those who have a taste for it?

So I like to think. But what do I think *about*? As the reader of these essays, taken from different publications over the last two decades, will find, there are a few themes that occur again and again. One is human consciousness and its evolution, both in the individual and in the culture at large. Another is that mysterious world that seems to strangely parallel our familiar, everyday one, the world of the occult, the magical, the esoteric. As you might suspect, these two themes overlap and are intimately related. There are aspects of what we call the occult that enter into states and forms of consciousness rather different from what we usually experience, just as certain unfamiliar modes of consciousness have a strangely magical character to them. One reason I became interested in the occult nearly forty years ago was precisely because it seemed to offer some way to approach the kind of *intensity* of consciousness I was instinctively seeking out—often in dangerous ways—just as it was through an interest in magic, the occult, and the esoteric that I found a way of mapping out the strange and unusual states I sometimes experienced, and which, it seems to me, suggest some latent possibilities waiting to be developed. Later, when I studied philosophy, I discovered that, while the kind of philosophy I encountered in university for the most part either ignored those aspects of reality in which I was most interested or dismissed them as nonsense, the "rejected" tradition of the occult, magic, and esotericism was more than open to them. Indeed, in many ways, it is precisely that tradition that has offered a home to these concerns, at least since the beginning of modern times. This is why, when I came to write, I wrote about ideas and people that generally fell into these areas—or, more broadly speaking, into the world of what we can call "alternative thought." (The fact that there were magazines and journals open to publishing my work also helped.)

The rather vague and capacious umbrella term "alternative thought" covers a wide range of subjects and individuals, connected by the fact that they do not find a place for themselves within the more narrow confines of modern, rationalist, scientistic thinking. This does not mean I am an enemy of science. Far from it; in fact for a time when I was first being published, I worked as a science writer for a major university in California. But I am a critic of the belief—for that is what it is—that the limited purview of materialistic science can explain everything in existence, and that what it can't explain is either unreal or unimportant. While it is an undoubted achievement to have secured a grasp on the Higgs boson, I object to the idea that in doing so we have "solved the mystery of the universe," as some of the news reports about the discovery announced. The universe is just as mysterious today as it was before the Higgs boson turned up. We may, indeed, have a firmer idea of *how* it hangs together, but we are no nearer to understanding *why* it is here in the first place and, more important, what we are supposed to do now that we find ourselves in it. Philosophy in the old school—going back to Plato and ending, perhaps, in the early twentieth century—used to address these questions, but in more recent years it has given them up. My sympathies are with the old school; the questions of why we exist and how we should live seem more important than what the next elementary particle in line to be discovered may be, certainly more important than the semantic nitpicking that much academic philosophy has descended into. Most of the people I write about in these essays thought so, too, and that, more than anything else, is why I am attracted to them. They were looking for the invisible, we could say, and so was I.

But what I found when I started to write about these ideas was that the lives of the people who held them were just as fascinating as the ideas themselves, and that a study of them provided a kind of counter-history to the one we are usually given. Almost half of my books are biographies. I've written studies of Emanuel Swedenborg, C. G. Jung,

P. D. Ouspensky, Rudolf Steiner, H. P. Blavatsky, and Aleister Crowley. For all my interest in the occult, the magical, and the esoteric, I am at heart an existentialist. Existentialism, of course, has nothing to do with the occult or, for that matter, with spirituality of any kind. As presented in thinkers like Sartre, Heidegger, and Camus, it is a grim affair, stoically affirming human freedom, limited as it is, in a contingent, accidental universe. But aside from the explicit beliefs—or lack of them—associated with existentialism, its essence is a concern with the *meaning* of human existence, a question that religion also used to address but which it seems to have mislaid some time ago. And this meaning, existentialism argues, cannot be discovered by sitting in an armchair and contemplating life. It can only be found by living—which, in any case, is unavoidable. What I found in writing about the lives of many of the people in this collection is that, as the writer Henry Miller once said, they "lived life to the hilt." These "revolutionaries of the soul," as my editor, Richard Smoley, calls them—hence the title of this book—not only thought about and questioned reality, they also threw themselves into it, often headfirst. They sought *more* out of life than what we usually settle for, and their revolutions embraced both the inner and outer worlds, broadening both in many ways. Madame Blavatsky hit the revolutionary barricades with Mazzini and Garibaldi. Ouspensky "remembered himself" during the chaos of World War I and the Bolshevik revolution. Jean Gebser nearly lost his life escaping from Franco's army in the Spanish Civil War. Jung descended into his unconscious while wrestling with psychosis, a struggle he shared with the playwright August Strindberg and the religious philosopher Swedenborg. Owen Barfield, with whom I had the good fortune to meet and speak with one afternoon some eighteen years ago, when I had first moved to London, saw more of the twentieth century than anyone else in this book, living through two world wars and ending his days contemplating the meaning of the information age. (He died not long after our meeting, at the age of ninety-nine, and I believe I conducted the last interview with him.) Rudolf Steiner avoided assassination by early proto-Nazis. Some, like the occult historian James

Webb, did not survive their encounter with chaos. Others, like the dark magician Aleister Crowley, swallowed enough experience for a dozen lives; while still others, like the occult scholar Manly P. Hall, succumbed, for all their erudition, to spiritual con men. These were not bloodless rationalists, sizing up life from a comfortable distance, but men and women who found themselves in the thick of it, as well as in dimensions of reality most of us rarely encounter. That they lived life to the hilt and then some, Henry Miller, I think, would have agreed.

Another aspect of this collection I'd like to point out is that many of the essays assume a broader, more literary-philosophical familiarity than what is usually the case in a book dealing with occultists and magicians. The article on Ouspensky, for example, places him in the literary world of 1930s London, and the one on the eccentric Polish explorer and ethnologist Jan Potocki centers on his single and singularly strange masterpiece, *The Manuscript Found in Saragossa*. Many readers, I suspect, are not that familiar with Jean Gebser, who combines a deep spirituality with the mandarin philosophical tradition of Central Europe. Much of Owen Barfield's philosophy is based on his study of poetry—as is Gebser's—and August Strindberg, of course, is one of the most important figures in literary modernism. Colin Wilson's examples for a new faculty of human consciousness come from some of the great writers of the last century. One of the problems with much of today's literature on spirituality is that it is too parochial, too limited in its context. It has become a genre, and it does not step over the borders of its niche too often. This is unfortunate. Market forces are probably to blame, with publishers and authors hesitant to confuse their readers ("Is this book about spirituality, or literature, or what?"), and the readers themselves more than likely want something simple and direct and not too challenging. This is a bad situation, and I for one make a point of appealing to readers' intelligence—smartening them up rather than dumbing them down—and of making them stretch their imagination, even if only a little. The questions that obsessed the people in this book (and its author) are not limited to one neatly squared-off patch of reality; and in any case, reality, as we know, is never neatly squared off. The question of the meaning and purpose of human existence is not the property of a few "experts" working in their limited fields; it pervades every aspect of our lives, and as I argue in my book *A Dark Muse* (2005) about the links between literature and the occult, some of the deepest spiritual questions in the last two centuries have been addressed as often by writers and poets as by more ostensibly "spiritual" figures—sometimes more often and more successfully, in fact. We need to return these questions to the broader fields of human endeavor instead of keeping them neatly tucked away in "mind, body, spirit" and other genres. If that means challenging ourselves, then let's be challenged. It's the only way the spirit grows. In fact, the growing interest in "occulture"—the meeting ground between the occult and culture—recognizes this fact, and in the past few years I have participated in several conferences and seminars dedicated to this idea in the United States, Europe, and the United Kingdom.

The essays are arranged in a rough chronological order—*rough* is the operative word, as some pieces fall out of sequence—and although I have edited here and there, neatening and correcting, I have kept them as much as possible in their original form. I have done so because this is not a book in the sense of having one theme, worked out chapter by chapter, but a collection of writings done at different times. There is some overlap and some minimal repetition, but this seemed to lend itself to a natural and unplanned continuity; it was while going over these essays and articles that I felt they were, in a way, reaching out to each other to form a kind of lattice. The one anachronistic arrangement is with the first essay, "Colin Wilson and Faculty X," one of the earliest pieces in the book, if not the earliest; it was first published twenty years ago. As readers of my work know, Wilson has been an enormous influence on me; it was through a reading of his book *The Occult* (1971)—still fascinating and important more than forty years later—that started me on my explorations into the occult and the hidden powers of consciousness. Sadly, Wilson, my mentor and friend whom I knew for thirty years, passed away in December 2013, while I was putting this collection together; he was eighty-two. Putting him at the start of this collection is a small tribute to the importance and significance that I, like many others, believe his work holds for the future of human evolution.

The last essay, "The Strange Death of James Webb," comes at the end for a different reason. Webb's tragic plight, his inability to completely accept or reject the occult, seems indicative of the situation our culture as a whole faces in regard to the occult. Our conscious, rational selves reject it as an outmoded superstition and see interest in it as evidence of a weak mind. Yet, as popular culture shows, the occult is still alive and well in our imaginations. We may reject it in the daylight, but in our dreams it comes to life.

So here are some revolutionaries of the soul. I hope they stir things up for you.

Gary Lachman
London, January 2014

CHAPTER ONE

Colin Wilson and Faculty X

There is a passage in Hermann Hesse's *Steppenwolf* that never fails to move me. The Steppenwolf, Harry Haller, a lonely, middle-aged intellectual, has spent an evening as he has spent other evenings, walking aimlessly through town, avoiding his room where awaits the product of his fruitless, listless days: the razor. Weary of avoiding his dismal fate, Harry enters a tavern for a brief respite and there drinks a glass of wine. Slowly his mood shifts. The process is gradual, but as he sips his wine, the Steppenwolf's thoughts expand, like a gas lighter than air. "A refreshing laughter rose in me," Harry tells us. "It soared aloft like a soap bubble, reflecting the whole world in miniature on its rainbow surface." He sinks into the warmth. Perhaps his fate is not so terrible. He meditates further still and slowly, hesitantly, looks into his soul. "In my brain," he says, "were stored a thousand pictures."

Harry thinks of an ancient weathered wall; of old, forgotten illuminated texts; of poems long gone to oblivion; of a solitary cypress on a forlorn hill; of the movement of clouds at night above the Rhine. A thousand thousand pictures come to him, more numerous than he can imagine, each one contributing its own secret import, its own special significance to the seeming absurdity and chaos of his life. Harry reflects on these and realizes that he is happy. "The golden trail was blazed. I was reminded of the eternal, of Mozart, and the stars." Harry wouldn't keep his appointment with the razor that night.

What exactly has happened? Has the Steppenwolf merely got drunk and forgotten his burden? Has the wine *obscured* something from his vision, namely the fact that he is a miserable middle-aged man who will

9

sooner or later slit his throat? Or does it *reveal* something that until then had been obscured? The same sort of experience happens again and again throughout the novel. Lying in bed with a woman after an evening of lovemaking, the ordinarily miserable Harry feels that "for moments together my heart stood still between delight and sorrow to find how rich was the gallery of my life, and how thronged the soul of the wretched Steppenwolf with high eternal stars and constellations." Does this sound like a man who wants to kill himself? What has happened?

Harry, the wretched Steppenwolf, has had an experience of what Colin Wilson calls "Faculty X." Harry may have known about all these things before, but now he *really* knows about them. This "really knowing" is the basic idea behind Wilson's philosophy.

Developed in his major studies on the paranormal—*The Occult* (1971), *Mysteries* (1978), and *Beyond the Occult* (1988)—and running through practically all his work, the central idea behind Wilson's notion of Faculty X is that it is a sense of *the reality of other times and places*. As Wilson points out, probably the most famous example of Faculty X—so called because we have yet to recognize it clearly and give it its own name—in modern literature is the opening of Marcel Proust's *Remembrance of Things Past* (1913–1927). There the narrator, Proust himself, tells of his curious experience eating his famous madeleine dipped in tea. Suddenly, from some dark forgotten psychic recess, the memory of his youth in Combray wells up in him, and it is as if he is there once again. The effect is tremendous; as Wilson writes, Proust had "ceased now to feel mediocre, contingent, mortal." Proust, too, suddenly realized the reality of his own life, and the rest of his eleven-hundred-page novel is an attempt to "recapture the past."

Another example comes from T. S. Eliot's "Ash Wednesday," where the poet writes that "the lost heart stiffens and rejoices for the lost sea air and the lost sea voices." This is essentially the same experience as Hesse and Proust describe: the sudden realization that the past really happened and that, in some strange way, it is just as real now as it was then. Which is another way of saying that reality, however we want to define it, is not confined to the present moment.

This is strange. As Wilson points out, we tend to believe that reality *is* confined to the present moment. This is why the realization of the *reality* of other times and places has such a profound effect on writers like Hesse, Proust, and Eliot. Clearly this suggests one thing: there is something wrong with our ideas about space and time.

If you hold a chicken's beak to the ground and draw a chalk line from its eyes, it will not move. When it comes to time, human beings are very much like paralyzed chickens: we seem to be stuck to a particular chalk line we call "now." The situation, Wilson argues, is absurd: human beings, he believes, are capable of transcending the limitations of the present moment and of achieving, as he calls it, a "mastery over time, as if every moment of your life could be recalled as clearly as the last ten minutes."

We have seen three of the most important figures in modern literature bear this speculation out. There is also evidence from science. As Wilson points out, one of the most fascinating discoveries about human memory came from the work of the neurologist Wilder Penfield. While operating on a patient, Penfield tested the effect of electrical stimulation of the temporal cortex. The result was astonishing. Penfield discovered that when the probe stimulated the patient's cortex, the patient would immediately be "sent back" to sometime in the past. (As neurosurgery is done without anesthetic—the brain feels no pain— patients were able to report their experiences.)

Penfield concluded that every moment of our lives is stored in some way in our brain and that if triggered by the proper stimulus—an electric probe or a piece of cake—we can relive these moments in vivid detail. We might say that the brain has a built-in virtual reality machine. We also remember the enduring belief that at the point of death people see their entire lives pass before them.

Wilson has his own ideas about the part the brain plays in Faculty X, an altogether easier and less cumbersome means of grasping the reality of other times and places than having a near-death experience or undergoing brain surgery. One of the most curious facts about human anatomy is that we have two brains. In *Frankenstein's Castle* (1980) Wilson discusses the split-brain research of Roger Sperry and Robert Ornstein. Its basic findings are well known: the left brain seems to control our logical functions, like language and mathematics, and the right our more intuitive powers. These have by now become a cliché: we say the left brain is a scientist, the right an artist. What seems less commonly known, Wilson suggests, is the strange fact that these two, the scientist and the artist, are literally two different people. You, reading these words, live in the left brain. In the right is a strange silent partner whom we call "the unconscious."

Most of *Frankenstein's Castle* deals with the interaction between the two sides of the brain. Wilson believes that the right brain is responsible for paranormal phenomena like synchronicities and for mystical experiences and the curious bursts of affirmation that the psychologist Abraham Maslow called "peak experiences." In a later book Wilson suggests the peculiar contribution that brain physiology may make to our question about the "reality" of other times and places. Relating how John Cowper Powys "appeared" one evening in the Manhattan apartment of his fellow novelist Theodore Dreiser while at the same time sitting in his cottage in upstate New York—a phenomenon the nineteenth-century psychic investigator Frederick Myers called "phantasms of the living"—Wilson writes:

> We take it for granted that we live in a "solid" world of space and time, advancing from moment to moment according to unchangeable laws, and that we are stuck in the place that we happen to be at the moment. We are, in a sense, "trapped." We feel this particularly strongly when we are bored or miserable—that we are helplessly at the mercy of this physical world into which we happen to have been born. Yet these odd experiences all seem to show that this is untrue. The "real you" is not trapped in space and time. With a certain kind of effort of will, it can rise above space and time and be "elsewhere."

Commenting on the fact that neuroscientists really have no idea *why* we should have two brains, Wilson goes on to make a remarkable suggestion:

> My own belief is that we have two brains so we can be in *two places at the same time*. Human beings are *supposed* to be capable of being in two places at the same time. Yet we have not quite discovered the "trick." When we do, we shall be a completely different kind of creature— no longer the same kind of human being who lives out his life so incompetently on this long-suffering planet, but something far more powerful and purposeful.

This is why Wilson believes that man is on the point of an evolutionary leap. But although paranormal phenomena like "phantasms of the living" offer some of the more spectacular evidence for our ability to be in two places at the same time, they are not the only support for Wilson's theory. There is other evidence. In a sense, you, as you read this essay, are in two places at once. In the first place, you are in whatever physical surroundings you happen to occupy. But in the second place, if I am doing my job correctly and have interested you in these ideas, you also occupy the world of thought and imagination, a world very much like the "elsewhere" Wilson speaks about.

In a very real sense, we are not trapped by space and time. Consider what happens when I take a book from my shelf, say a volume of history. I open it, flip through the pages, idly glance at a paragraph or two, not really reading but just skimming the surface. Then something catches my eye, say a description of ancient Athens or a remark about the Peloponnesian War. I focus more intently on the page and sink back in my chair with the intention to read through the section. A minute passes, then two. I'm "interested." I forget the solid world I've just been contemplating and the ubiquitous moment I've just occupied. Suddenly, almost imperceptibly, the world has changed. The solid walls have disappeared, and in their place I am hovering over vast stretches of time. I read on. Now, if I am relaxed enough and can muster the concentration, something strange may happen. A particularly well-written passage may trigger it, or I may not be able to link it to any specific cause, but I will suddenly be aware that these events *really* happened. I don't know another way to put it. I am suddenly catapulted back in time, as Proust was to Combray, and am jolted by the recognition that whatever it is I am reading about—the trial of Socrates or the battle of Thermopylae—actually took place. It isn't just words, a collection of facts, bare details: it's real.

Faculty X is this strange capacity we have to feel the reality of times and places beyond that of the present moment, to literally be "in two places at once." And the obvious thing is that, except for certain moments, the physical place I occupy is altogether less important, less fascinating and interesting, than the mental "place." This has been known for ages. The *Tao Te Ching* says that "without going out of my door, I can know all things on earth. Without looking out of my window, I can know all things in heaven. The farther one travels, the less one knows."

Now of course there are many instances in which physical location is extremely important: one shouldn't daydream too deeply while driving a car. And the physical space of some unfortunate people is so miserable it is more important to remedy that than it is to float off into dream worlds of the imagination. But we also know that once we are in a physical space that doesn't demand our attention, the first thing we do is find something to occupy ourselves besides the four walls.

An animal is content with merely occupying a physical space. If no one plays with it and nothing else arouses its attention, a cat will stare into space and sooner or later fall asleep. Many of us find watching television an appalling pastime, but compared to a cat's incapacity to be in two places at once, the viewers of the worst sitcom are virtually Prousts and Steppenwolves. As far as we can tell, it seems that animals simply lack this ability. Even our slang recognizes that the capacity to take imaginative voyages is a sign of evolutionary advance. When someone sits at home and does very little—like watching television—we say he or she is "vegetating," clearly a recognition that such a person has slipped below a truly human level.

A well-known book of the early 1970s by Ram Dass admonished its readers to *Be Here Now*. While I can understand and sympathize with the good intentions and valuable psychology behind this maxim, it is also true that in a very real sense, to "be here now" is something that imaginative human beings simply find a bore.

Why does having two brains allow us to be in two places at once? After all, I may have two brains, but they are in one skull. Wilson suggests an answer. When both brains are working properly, when the artist and the scientist collaborate, then the sense of reality, that feeling that some incident in my past—or in that of the entire race, for that matter—*really happened* occurs. Why is this? The answer lies in the powers of the different cerebral hemispheres. Human beings are the dominant species on the planet because of the left brain's ability to focus on the details of experience. Yet this dominance has come at a price. In learning to focus on details, we have to a great extent forgotten our ability to perceive overall patterns. We must imagine the scientist in the left brain peering at the world through a microscope. This focus enables us to gain greater control over nature than any other animal, but it has also landed us in a universe that often seems utterly meaningless. This is because the right brain, which is responsible for pattern recognition, is also the seat of our sense of meaning.

Think again of the act of reading. Were you to focus solely on the individual words of this sentence, its meaning would escape you. To understand it, you need to stand back from it, to see it and the paragraph and page and article as a whole. Wilson uses the analogy of a newspaper photograph. If you look through a magnifying glass at a photograph in the *New York Times*, you wouldn't see a picture at all, merely a series of dots. To recognize the figures in the photograph you need to stand back from it. This is what happened to Harry Haller when he drank his wine and was reminded of Mozart and the stars. Harry the intellectual looks at the world through a magnifying glass, seeing an enormous amount of detail, but lacking a sense of the overall pattern. This is why he finds the world such a gruesome place.

The left brain is oriented to "dealing" with the world; and although we are not all Harry Hallers, most of us confront experience with a habit of suspicion and caution that keeps us in a state of hypertension. To draw on the reading analogy once again, when we read something in a hurry, we generally comprehend little and retain less. When Harry sits in the café and sips his wine, his left brain begins to slow down. No longer in a hurry, it allows the right brain to do its work of supplying an overall sense of pattern and meaning, with the result that Harry suddenly remembers the reality of his life, not its mere facts, and is overwhelmed with the feeling of a tremendous discovery.

But, Wilson argues, we shouldn't jump to the conclusion that the left brain is a villain and the right a hero, a mistake many Romantic writers and artists of the nineteenth and twentieth centuries made. It is true that the right brain is the source of our sense of meaning. But as Wilson writes in *Frankenstein's Castle* and *Access to Inner Worlds* (1983), the remarkable thing is that the right brain seems to take its cues from the left. Through a study of hypnotism and of the work of Max Freedom Long on the teachings of the Hawaiian shamans known as kahunas, Wilson came to the conclusion that, contrary to Romantic ideas that see the left-brain ego as a villain to be got rid of by any means possible—drink, drugs, sex, violence—it is actually the boss when it comes to consciousness. The problem is that it doesn't know it's the boss. The left-brain ego, Wilson concluded, isn't too strong, as the Romantics argued; it's *too weak*.

It is true that the right brain is the source of power and capable of tremendous feats, ranging from the ability of idiots savants to determine almost instantly whether or not a six-digit number is prime, to the kinds of experience discussed earlier in this essay. Wilson contends that the unconscious looks to the ego for its direction. Without the left brain's sense of purpose and motivation, the right can easily sink into mental lethargy.

Many have sought to achieve higher consciousness through some means of deadening the left-brain ego, through psychedelic drugs, for example. Psychedelic drugs can "open the doors of perception," as Aldous Huxley, quoting William Blake, well knew. But Huxley also realized that "if everyone took mescaline, there would be no wars, but there would be no civilization either," because we would lack the motivation to create it. Left-brain-dominant consciousness reveals a world without meaning; right-brain-dominant consciousness reveals a world overflowing with meaning but inhibits our capacity to organize it. The answer, it seems, is to have both brains work together. This is Faculty X.

When the right brain supplies the meaning, then the facts of our existence take on a remarkable character. It is then that, like Proust, Hesse, and Eliot, we feel we are remembering something that we already know, but now *really* know. Faculty X is not a nostalgia for "times past" but an unrecognized power we have of *knowing* the world, almost like a sixth sense. And according to Wilson, it is a sense we can develop.

Although Proust devoted his life to recapturing the past, he wasn't confident that it could be done, at least not through conscious effort. "It is a labor in vain to attempt to recapture it," he wrote. "All the efforts of our intellect must prove futile." Everything depends, Proust believed, on some chance encounter triggering the unconscious memory—a bit of cake dipped in tea, or, later in the book, a loose paving stone. Yet this seems a curious assertion when we recall that Proust also remarked, after unsuccessful attempts to again trigger his memory through sips of tea, that "it is plain that the truth I am seeking lies not in the cup but in myself." Proust seems not to have followed this insight.

Wilson is more optimistic. He is confident that consciousness can soar above the limits of the present moment. In fact, Wilson believes it is a mistake to think of Faculty X as an unusual phenomenon. We have got into the habit of believing that reality is limited to the present moment only because we have got into the habit of taking a passive attitude toward our mental states. The truth is that Faculty X is really consciousness doing its proper work, which is, Wilson tells us, reaching out and *grabbing* reality.

Developing the insights of the philosopher Edmund Husserl, Wilson argues that the key to Faculty X, and indeed to all mental states, is an effort of will, what Husserl called "intentionality." It is true that Faculty X can come to us unexpectedly—practically all our experiences of it now happen in this way—but Wilson believes that we can develop a greater capacity to experience Faculty X by maintaining an attitude of optimism and purpose. In other words, by showing the right brain we mean business. Usually we are so weak and vacillating that the right brain, which holds the purse strings on our power supply, ignores us and falls asleep. Only in moments of crisis does it wake up and supply the left brain with energy. This is why so many of the individuals Wilson calls "Outsiders" actually sought out crisis (it was Wilson's first book, *The Outsider*, that launched him on his career in 1956, at the age of twenty-four). They knew instinctively that threat or emergency snaps us to attention and compels consciousness to work properly. "Living dangerously," as Nietzsche put it, has its drawbacks, but the insight to be gleaned from it is invaluable. If the right brain will respond to crisis, then it should be made to respond without crisis, *if* the left brain can convince the right that it is serious.

But there is a problem. As mentioned earlier, the right brain looks to the left for clues to how it should respond to a situation. But what kind of messages do we—the left brain—usually send it? Unless we are saints or perfected masters, we generally spend most of our time complaining about life, with the result that the right brain, which, Wilson says, tends to overreact to messages from the left, curls up into a ball, or worse, floods the left with waves of despair. (Oddly, the right brain tends to be pessimistic and depressive, the left optimistic and manic.) When this goes on for too long, we end up like Harry Haller, cursing our dismal fate and doing our best to avoid the razor. The first step in developing our capacity for Faculty X, then, is to create a sense of optimism—not about anything in particular, but a general sense that life means well by us, what Jean Gebser called "primal trust."

And this leads naturally to the next step, developing a sense of purpose. After we stop sending our right brain messages of doom, the next step is to foster a sense of *interest*. Mystics and poets tell us that we live in a fascinating universe, a cosmos of such complexity that it seems unthinkable anyone could be bored in it. Yet this is exactly what happens. Our whole obsession with youth is based on the idea that, after a certain age, life loses its appeal and we spend the rest of our days doing "the same old thing." But when we look at creative individuals, like the playwright Bernard Shaw, who continued working into his nineties, and the poet W. B. Yeats, who threw off his youthful pessimism and grew into a giant of world literature in his later years, we see that modern culture's emphasis on the emptiness of life is an enormous mistake, based on a complete misunderstanding about the nature of consciousness. The only way to prove this, of course, is to actually develop our capacity for Faculty X, which really means developing our power to grasp reality.

If the past really continues to exist in the present, as Proust, Hesse, and Eliot seem to show, then our belief that reality is only what occupies us at the moment is a bad habit we need to outgrow. We are simply not in touch with all of reality when we forget about the vast *objective* world outside the present. This idea really shouldn't seem strange; after all, we don't believe that the rest of the spatial world ceases to exist when we shut the door to our room. If we think of Faculty X spatially, most of us are very short-sighted people who occasionally have a brief but vivid glimpse of the Grand Canyon or the Alps. If Colin Wilson is correct, we may be able to improve our eyesight so that we can take in these vistas at will.

Discovering Swedenborg

O ne of the most remarkable figures in modern European history
is the Swedish scientist, philosopher, and religious thinker
Emanuel Swedenborg (1688–1772). An Enlightenment intellectual who
combined a genius for invention with an incisive theoretical mind;
an inveterate traveler who combed Europe in search of scientific and
philosophical knowledge; a statesman who was also a student of the
Kabbalistic arts and who wedded a fascination with mystical eroticism
to the machinations of a secret agent—these characteristics alone
would qualify him as a figure of great interest. Yet Swedenborg's most
remarkable claim to fame was the series of profound psychological and
spiritual crises he experienced in his mid-fifties, which resulted in an
encounter with Jesus Christ and the first of many journeys to heaven,
hell, and the "spirit world," described in his book *Heaven and Hell*. Such
claims usually lead to a stint in the madhouse, but the many creative
men and women influenced by Swedenborg include Charles Baudelaire,
August Strindberg, W. B. Yeats, Aldous Huxley, Helen Keller, Jorge Luis
Borges, Czeslaw Milosz, Arnold Schoenberg, Honoré de Balzac, and
C. G. Jung. For Ralph Waldo Emerson, Swedenborg was a "mastodon
of literature"; and the Nobel Prize-winning scientist Svante Arrhenius
recognized that his contributions to science included, among other
things, the nebula theory of planetary and solar formation.

Yet most people, if they're aware of Swedenborg, know vaguely that he
was the inspiration for an eccentric form of Christianity that numbered
among its followers William Blake and that usually gets placed on the
cultural map just beyond Jehovah's Witnesses. Or that he provided

some of the most convincing examples of precognition, telepathy, and communication with the dead, bravura displays of psychic phenomena recounted in practically every history of the paranormal. This was more or less my own take until I became more acquainted with Swedenborg's life. While writing *A Dark Muse* (2005), a book about writers and the occult, I discovered that many of the occult ideas permeating modern Western literature had their source in Swedenborg. This discovery struck me as important—important enough to accept a commission to write a book about this little-known genius. What I found out along the way was surprising. With any luck, this brief account of the "other" Swedenborg will prompt some readers to make some similar discoveries for themselves.

Swedenborg was born Emanuel Swedberg to a prosperous Stockholm family on January 29, 1688; the family later changed their name to Swedenborg when they were ennobled in 1719. Emanuel's father, Jesper Swedberg, was a regimental chaplain who would later be appointed a bishop. His mother, Sara Behm, a wealthy mine owner, was the daughter of an official in the Swedish Board of Mines. Swedenborg had a happy childhood, but he also had experiences he couldn't share with his siblings. As a child Swedenborg had visions. His unseen "playmates" spoke to him, and when he repeated what they said, his parents were astounded. When asked who had told him these things, Swedenborg answered that he had heard them from the boys he played with in the family's garden house. His parents knew he had been alone and decided that angels must be speaking through him, a presage of the extraordinary communications to come.

The young Swedenborg developed a skill he would put to great use throughout his life. During his morning and evening prayers, he learned how to control his breath so that it seemed he was hardly breathing. This later became an awareness of the intimate relation between breath and concentration, or, in physiological terms, the lungs and the brain, one of his many intuitions about the functioning of the body that would later be established by medical science. Swedenborg's "search for the soul," the scientific pursuit that occupied the first half of his life, led through the brain, and through it he arrived at several insights that modern science has since discovered, one being the "coincidence of the motion of the brain with respiration." It's also more than coincidental that regulated breathing, and the chemical changes in the brain accompanying it, has for centuries been a tested means of entering altered states of consciousness.

When Swedenborg was fourteen, his father was made a bishop, and in 1703 the family moved to Brunsbo. Emanuel, however, didn't go. He was enrolled at Uppsala University, and it was decided he should stay and continue his studies. He moved in with his older sister Anna and her husband, Erik Benzelius. Benzelius, the university librarian, was a brilliant man, and he became the boy's mentor. He introduced Swedenborg to science, and it's also possible that Swedenborg had his first encounter with the occult tradition through his brother-in-law. Benzelius was an Hebraist, and he knew F. M. van Helmont, who had annotated Christian Knorr von Rosenroth's *Kabbala denudata* (The Kabbalah unveiled), a central occult text. Hebrew was highly prized among Benzelius's peers, not only because it was the language of the Old Testament, but also because it was the language in which the books of Kabbalah, the Jewish mystical tradition, communicated the secrets of the Divine. Benzelius had also met the philosopher Gottfried Wilhelm von Leibniz, who, it is alleged, had become a member of a secret Rosicrucian society in 1667; years later, Swedenborg would try unsuccessfully to meet Leibniz himself. (Curiously, one of the most noted scientist-philosophers of the time, René Descartes, was suspected of being a Rosicrucian.) Benzelius was a strong supporter of Descartes's ideal of free inquiry. Jesper Swedberg, however, vehemently opposed it, and for much of his student years, Swedenborg was torn between his growing love of science and duty to his father's beliefs.

Benzelius advised Swedenborg to travel and study science abroad; England, in particular, was the place to go. Swedenborg's father, however, wouldn't finance the trip. With his schooling finished, Emanuel had moved to his father's house, but he found the place deadening. He was fascinated by the work of Sweden's most famous scientist and inventor, Christopher Polhem, and believed that his destiny lay in following his path. Benzelius agreed, and he convinced Polhem as well, who was willing to accept Swedenborg as an assistant. The only problem was that Swedenborg was nowhere to be found. Soon they discovered he was in England.

Aside from his first taste of travel and freedom, Swedenborg's English adventure, the first of many journeys, provided an experience that left a lasting impression. Just outside London, some Swedes boarded the ship and persuaded Swedenborg to accompany them. But the plague had broken out in Sweden, and the English had commanded the passengers to remain in quarantine. Swedenborg broke the quarantine, the penalty for which was hanging. He was caught and just barely escaped the noose, but the virtue of a "bill of health"—an essential item in those days—stayed with him and would return in the context of a very different crisis many years ahead.

London became an important place for Swedenborg. He lodged in the city on six occasions and spent his last days there. London was also the scene for his initial entry into the spirit worlds and for a peculiarly eerie vision in which he was advised by an angel "not to indulge the belly too much." It's possible that during his first visit, Swedenborg was initiated into a Jacobite Masonic lodge and became involved in a Franco-Swedish Masonic conspiracy to restore the Stuarts to the English throne. It was also in London that Swedenborg may have come under the influence of the rabbi Samuel Jacob Chayyim Falk, who numbered among his other students the famous mage Alessandro Cagliostro. Falk is a mysterious figure; it may be that he is one of the "unknown superiors" that W. B. Yeats, in his reminiscences of his time as a member of the Hermetic Order of the Golden Dawn, refers to when speaking of the order's history. Falk was at the hub of occult life in London at the time Swedenborg made his later visits, as well as during his last days there. Falk set up an alchemical laboratory on London Bridge and, from his house in the East End, ran an esoteric school. An occult community of Freemasons, Kabbalists, Rosicrucians, and alchemists, as well as the followers of the eccentric Count Nikolaus von Zinzendorf, leader of the Moravian Brethren, gathered around Falk, and it is very possible that Swedenborg moved in this circle.

One aspect of the Moravians seems to have interested Swedenborg very much. Some of their doctrines were borrowed from Kabbalah, as well as from the followers of Sabbatai Zevi, the false Messiah. Part of the Sabbatian worship involved sex, and it's possible that the several erotic entries in Swedenborg's diaries reflect his participation in Count Zinzendorf's Sabbatian-Kabbalistic rites. Although Swedenborg remained a bachelor, sex was always an important ingredient in his philosophy, and he had some very liberal ideas about it: he kept mistresses and advocated concubinage and pre- and extramarital relations. One of his last books, *Conjugial* [*sic*] *Love*, or *Marriage Love*, was written when he was eighty and depicts the delights of heavenly eroticism. In Swedenborg's heaven, men and women find their true partners, who are not always the ones they knew on earth, and their sexual lives continue; in fact, they're supposed to get even better.

Along with his Kabbalistic studies, Swedenborg devoted himself to mathematics, mechanics, and astronomy. In his travels he tended to take rooms with craftsmen so that he could learn their trades: watchmaking, cabinetry, brass working, marble inlay. In London he invested in many scientific instruments: prisms, microscopes, scales, quadrants, a camera obscura, an air pump. His letters to Benzelius were read by the Guild of the Curious, the first Swedish scientific society, who wrote back asking him to make contact with John Flamsteed, the Astronomer Royal. Later, Swedenborg's letters would help him become the editor of the first Swedish scientific journal, *Daedalus hyperboreus* (The northern Daedalus). It was also in London that he began what would become an almost lifelong pursuit. Swedenborg had a burning desire for fame, and he was determined to win the prize offered by Greenwich Observatory to devise a method of establishing longitude at sea; he lost out when

John Harrison produced the chronometer. After London he went to Oxford, where he met the astronomer Edmund Halley, discoverer of the comet.

One of Swedenborg's letters contained a list of proposed inventions, including a submarine, an aqueduct, a machine gun, a do-it-yourself home entertainment center, an automobile, and an airplane. The Europe Swedenborg was intent on conquering was awakening to a delight in mechanized marvels, such as Jacques de Vaucason's flute-playing android and mechanical excreting duck, and Wolfgang von Kempelen's mechanical chess-playing Turk. Philip James de Loutherberg, Swedenborg's friend and later the acquaintance of William Blake, would become famous for the lighting and sound effects he created for David Garrick's theater in Drury Lane. However, none of Swedenborg's ideas got beyond his imagination: true to form, his father mislaid all of the drawings and calculations for his machines.

In January 1716 Swedenborg went to work with Polhem, staying with him for three years, putting his mechanical skill to great use. In 1717 the Swedish king Karl XII commissioned Polhem to build a dry dock at Karlskrona; Swedenborg met the king and, at Polhem's request, Karl XII appointed Swedenborg a special assessor on Sweden's Board of Mines. Other important projects Swedenborg tackled were the locks on the Trollhättan Canal, linking Stockholm with the North Sea; Sweden's first salt works; and a remarkable feat of engineering, in which Swedenborg managed to move the king's navy some fifteen miles across land in order to defeat the Norwegians at Fredrikshald. In 1718 Karl XII died from a bullet to the head during the siege—it's unclear whether the shot came from a Norwegian or a Swedish gun—and with the king's death, Swedenborg's career as an engineer, and his association with Polhem, ended.

Swedenborg's real passion, his "ruling love" as he would later call it, was for something larger than invention and applied science. He was obsessed with the big questions: the meaning of life, the structure of the cosmos, where infinity ended. His work as assessor of mines seems like something of a cover. After leaving Polhem, Swedenborg took up his responsibilities as a member of the Swedish Diet. In 1719 the new queen, Ulrika Eleonora, ennobled the families of Sweden's bishops (this was when the Swedbergs became Swedenborgs) and Emanuel took his seat in the House of Nobles. He contributed important papers on a number of issues, fulfilled his duties as a statesman, and was an exemplary assessor, but his heart and mind lay elsewhere.

In 1734, when he was forty-six, Swedenborg published his first major scientific work, a three-volume opus entitled *The Mineral Kingdom*. Parts two and three were technical mineralogical treatises, dealing with the mining of iron and copper. Part one, *The Principles of Natural Things*, or *The Principia*, was devoted to more metaphysical pursuits. Here Swedenborg offered a theory about the nature of the universe. He also explored the question of how the finite, physical world can originate in an infinite, immaterial source, that is, God. This was the beginning of Swedenborg's long quest to find a scientific proof of the soul.

Swedenborg saw the limitations of the new science rising out of the work of Newton and Descartes. Newtonian science was content to formulate laws out of the evidence offered to the senses, but Swedenborg was determined to get behind sensory phenomena in order to arrive at their causes. "The sign that we are willing to be wise," he wrote, "is the desire to know the causes of things, and to investigate the secret and unknown operations of nature." For the next decade Swedenborg did just that.

Swedenborg was aided in this quest by a strange psychological quirk. In his next major work, *The Economy of the Animal Kingdom* (also translated as *The Dynamics of the Soul's Domain*), Swedenborg speaks of a peculiar inner experience. Whenever he felt he was approaching some discovery, Swedenborg saw a "certain cheering light and joyful confirmatory brightness" that played around the sphere of his mind, "a kind of mysterious radiation that darts through some sacred temple in the brain." This "confirmatory brightness" returned to Swedenborg whenever his meditations brought him closer to the truth, and he referred to it as "the sign."

Some of Swedenborg's speculations seem well ahead of their time. In *The Principia*, Swedenborg posited "dimensionless points" as the building blocks of the universe. Having no dimensions, they have no extension in space. Not limited to one location, they are universally present, existing everywhere. Given this, every portion of our spatiotemporal world can serve as a starting point for a process of inference, which will then lead to the infinite. Within this, all of the apparently separate elements of our world exist in a kind of seamless unity. In recent times, a similar idea was developed by the physicist David Bohm, with his notion of an "implicate order" formed of "unbroken wholeness." Another similar contemporary development is holograms. Like Swedenborg's points, the image in a hologram isn't localized: it's contained in every part of the whole.

Swedenborg's points are also reminiscent of fractals. Swedenborg saw his points as the connecting link to the infinite; as such, they had access to infinite energy, an intuition echoed by later insights into particle physics. This infinite energy is constrained by the points, and the points themselves suffer a further constraint by being compelled to move in definite directions. The movement of Swedenborg's points over time forms a particle, and its collective movements are seen as an atom. The atoms eventually form larger bodies. Swedenborg continues to repeat this pattern, eventually arriving at very large bodies like the sun, which he envisions as being made up of many smaller images of itself, much like a hologram or fractal. This reiterative element in Swedenborg's system is an example of "like-partedness," and we can just as easily say that, for Swedenborg, the sun is made up of innumerable infinitesimal suns as we can that, for him, the sun is really just an immense particle. This idea would repeat itself in Swedenborg's later theological writings, when he speaks of the universe as a Great Man, of which we are all parts. Similarly, Swedenborg's heaven is made up of angels. This is an idea common to Hermetic thought, its basic formula being the alchemical maxim "as above, so below."

Swedenborg's hypothesis produced other remarkable anticipations. He projected the spiraling of his dimensionless points out into the cosmos, and his picture of the Milky Way as a great wheel of stars anticipated our modern concepts of the galaxy. The French mathematician Pierre Simon de Laplace is usually given this honor, but there's a good chance that Swedenborg should be credited with first positing the nebula theory of solar and planetary formation. His other suggestions include the ideas that the earth and other planets have gradually removed themselves from the sun and received a lengthening time of revolution; that the earth's rotation has been gradually increased; that the galaxies themselves are arranged in greater systems; that stars have axial rotation; that planets are formed by the ring of stellar material given off by novae; and that some stars, which we now call pulsars, emit pulses of radiation.

In later years, Swedenborg spoke about life on other planets. This suggests one further contemporary cosmological anticipation, the "anthropic cosmological principle." In its strong form, it argues that, in our universe, intelligent life forms like ourselves *must* arise. Swedenborg takes this even further: the universe was created *in order for* beings like ourselves to exist. This is so because it is through beings like ourselves that heaven is populated. The inhabitants of one planet alone wouldn't suffice for this purpose, so the cosmos is littered with other planets harboring human life.

In 1737 Swedenborg traveled to Paris and Italy to study anatomy and physiology. He also read widely in the anatomical literature of the time. This study produced his writings on the brain, posthumously published as *The Cerebrum*. Another product was *The Economy of the Animal Kingdom*. This work has nothing to do with animals in the wild: the "kingdom" is the human body and the "animal," the animating energy, or soul. Here Swedenborg made his final assault on locating the elusive "seat of the soul." This was not an uncommon pursuit; Descartes himself had argued that the soul was lodged in the pineal gland. But Swedenborg had his own ideas, and his work shows how ahead of his time he was. In *The Cerebrum*, Swedenborg made his most important contribution to neuroscience: the recognition that the gray matter of the cerebral cortex houses higher psychic functions like consciousness and thought, something that wouldn't be "officially" recognized until more than a century later. Some of Swedenborg's other insights include the existence of the cerebrospinal fluid, the circulation of the cerebrospinal fluid through interstices between the fibers and nerves of the body, and the existence of the central canal of the spinal cord. He also perceived that the central ganglia and spinal ganglia take over some of the movement initiations of the cerebrum (conditioned reflexes); that the optic lobes are connected with the sense of sight; that the function of the brain is partly as a "chemical laboratory" distributing chemicals through the pituitary gland; that the blood is being continually broken down and replaced; that the quality of the blood depends upon the organ and the person; that the smallest organic particles (what he called "fibers" and "cortical elements") are independent centers of forces endowed with individual life; and that each organ and "fiber" selects its own requisite nutrients from the blood supplied by the heart's pumping action—i.e., the blood plasma is not *forced* into the tissues but rather is *drawn in* selectively by the tissues themselves.

We can add that Swedenborg was the first to recognize the existence and importance of neurons and that early on he emphasized the significance of the frontal lobes for the higher psychic functions. A further insight into the brain appeared in Swedenborg's later career, when the doors of the spirit world were opened to him and he observed that the geography of heaven corresponds to that of the human body: Swedenborg anticipated the findings of split-brain research, delegating the "rational" to the left side of the brain and the "affections or things of the will" to the right. Swedenborg also gave importance to the cerebellum, a kind of proto-cerebrum located in the back of the skull. It is through the cerebellum that the influx from the divine enters the soul. (That's why, in heaven, no one is allowed to stand behind an angel.)

Swedenborg's suggestion that the cerebellum is a contact point between the human and the divine was echoed centuries later by the psychologist Stan Gooch, who saw the cerebellum as the seat of paranormal and mystical experience. Gooch's suggestion that Neanderthal man possessed a larger cerebellum and was hence more "mystical" than we are parallels Swedenborg's belief that, in an earlier time, humankind was closer to the Divine and could perceive its presence directly. Gooch suggested that individuals with psychic powers would possess larger, more active cerebellums, and he came across one individual who "reported *actual conscious experience of the cerebellum during . . . paranormal activity.*" (Emphasis here and in other quotes are in the original unless otherwise noted.) The individual was Swedenborg.

Yet for all his discoveries about the brain, Swedenborg's search for a proof of the soul was coming up empty. The soul eluded all his efforts to locate it. Rather than accept this as proof that it didn't exist, as most scientists would, Swedenborg recognized the inadequacy of one of science's most cherished beliefs: the continuity of nature. Nature, this concept says, is of a piece, and the same laws accommodating physical reality should be applied to anything else. Swedenborg jettisoned this dogma and instead developed what he called "The Doctrine of Series and Degrees." There were, he saw, "breaks" in nature, "jumps," the kind of "explanatory gaps" that some contemporary philosophers see between the physical structure of the brain and the immaterial phenomena of consciousness. (No one has yet shown how we get from a neuron to a thought.) The idea also has some resonance with the notion of "punctuated equilibrium," which suggests that evolution doesn't operate gradually, but in sudden "leaps." For Swedenborg this was a tremendous insight, and it initiated a period of much soul searching of a different kind. For all his brilliance and questing intellect, he saw that science would not lead him to the soul, and this led to a protracted struggle between the heart and the head. This conflict between the religious and rational sides of his psyche, begun years before, reached a momentous climax on the night of April 6–7, 1744.

Swedenborg had already gone through a long period of strange dreams and trance states in which he "heard speech that no human tongue can utter," and felt agonies of "wretchedness as of final condemnation." He experienced spells of swooning, fainting, and uncontrollable trembling and days of "double thoughts," when an idea was immediately countered by its opposite. When Swedenborg went to bed that night, he heard a noise under his head; then, suddenly, a violent shuddering and a sound like thunder shook him. A great rush of wind threw him to the floor, and he seems to have had an out-of-body experience. He asked Christ to make him worthy of his grace, then he felt a hand grasp his, and he found himself in Christ's bosom. Christ asked Swedenborg if he had a "bill of health"—an allusion to Swedenborg's close shave with a hangman's noose on his first trip to London. Swedenborg answered that Christ knew the answer to this better than he did, to which Christ answered, "Well, then do." Later, this figure appeared again and told Swedenborg that he had chosen him to reveal the true meaning of scripture. In his last years, Swedenborg described this encounter to a friend:

> That same night were opened to me so that I became thoroughly convinced of their reality, the worlds of spirits, heaven, and hell, and I recognized there many acquaintances of every condition in life. From that day I gave up the study of all worldly science, and labored in spiritual things, according as the Lord commanded me to write. Afterwards the Lord opened, daily very often, my bodily eyes, so that, in the middle of the day I could see into the other world, and in a state of perfect wakefulness converse with angels and spirits.

Whatever we make of this transformation—and the arguments for Swedenborg's madness are no more eloquent than those for his spiritual genius—it is clear that, even without his journeys to heaven and hell, Swedenborg remains a figure of fascination and well worthy of discovery. His life and work, it seems to me, are emblematic of the need today for science to push beyond its artificial boundaries, erected by a willful limitation of its criteria for "evidence." Swedenborg was not the only scientist to recognize that science alone could not account for the mysteries of human existence. Alfred Wallace, codiscoverer with Charles Darwin of the theory of evolution through natural selection, believed that random mutations and environmental pressures by themselves could not account for man's moral urges and posited some "overruling intelligence" slowly guiding human beings in their spiritual development. Like Swedenborg, William James, who practically invented the science of psychology, devoted years of effort and energy toward discovering some "proof" of the soul. And John Eccles, who won the Nobel Prize in 1963 for his work on the brain's synapses, agreed with Swedenborg that the mind could not be reduced to some epiphenomenon of gray matter and argued, along with the philosopher Karl Popper, in favor of the irreducible reality of the Self. All these men were rigorous scientists, yet they all discovered that the most important things about human existence—consciousness, the mind, the self, free will—eluded even the most methodical investigation. Yet, unlike other scientists, they took this as evidence, not of their nonexistence, but of science's own limitations. Swedenborg surely went further in his spiritual pursuits; and the moral and existential value of his visionary ideas, which I have not even touched on here (I discuss them in my 2012 book *Swedenborg: An Introduction to His Life and Ideas*), may, for some, be what is truly important about him. We may take or leave them as we wish. For me, Swedenborg is worth discovering for the example he gives of a truly remarkable mind refusing to abandon its quest for the spiritual in man.

CHAPTER THREE

Jan Potocki and the
Saragossa Manuscript

Most English readers know the eccentric Count Jan Potocki as the author of one of the strangest works of nineteenth-century European literature, *The Manuscript Found in Saragossa* (1815). The *Saragossa Manuscript*, as it is often called, is a weird farrago of stories within stories, with an overall supernatural bent, modeled in many ways on *The Arabian Nights*. Over a period of sixty-six days, the young Walloon officer Alphonse van Worden recounts his adventures with gypsies, Kabbalists, demons, corpses, astrologers, the Wandering Jew, and secret societies. The work has rightly earned Potocki a place in the ranks of the great writers of supernatural fiction.

Born in 1761 to one of Poland's wealthiest aristocratic families, by the end of his life the famed traveler, ethnologist, linguist, and fantasist had become something of a superman. In an insatiable quest for knowledge, Potocki combined Enlightenment rationalism with a Romantic appetite for the strange and uncanny. Fantastic journeys, political intrigues, and arcane scholarship filled a career that can be best described as "Baron Munchausen meets Marco Polo." Educated at Geneva and Lausanne, the young count received a solid grounding in classical knowledge and soon revealed an astonishing capacity for languages, of which he spoke eight fluently, including Arabic. Then came training at the Vienna Academy of Military Engineering, followed by a stint of service to the Knights of Malta, which included a sea battle against the Barbary corsairs.

Potocki traveled widely at this time, making his way across Western Europe as well as journeying to Tunisia, Constantinople, Egypt, and Morocco. In Morocco he tried unsuccessfully to locate a manuscript of the original *Arabian Nights*, which enjoyed something of a craze in eighteenth-century Europe. While in Constantinople, he observed the traditional storytellers plying their trade. Their exotic accounts of adventure and mystery inspired him to turn his hand to a tale or two, which he included in his lively writings about his journeys. In Constantinople he also met Osman, his Turkish valet, who, from then on, accompanied the count everywhere for the rest of his life. Potocki also took to wearing oriental dress at this time and was often seen in a fez or burnoose. Along with his travel writings, Potocki pursued historical, cultural, and linguistic research wherever he found himself, thereby helping to found the discipline of ethnology.

In the mid-1780s, Potocki found himself in Paris, where he hobnobbed with Enlightenment figures in the salons and cafés of prerevolutionary France. It was here that he became involved in strange mystical intrigues, which some conspiracy theorists, like the splenetic Abbé Barruel, believed were responsible for the revolution itself. This was the Paris of Cagliostro, Swedenborg, and Mesmer, of Adam Weishaupt and the Bavarian Illuminati, of Kabbalism, séances, and Freemasonry, where followers of Martinez de Pasqually and the Order of the Elect Cohens mixed with the weird novelist Jacques Cazotte and the Hermetic philosopher Louis Claude de Saint-Martin.

In this atmosphere of magic, mysticism, and secret societies, the young Potocki was intoxicated by the heady brew of esotericism and progress in a way that would later inform his single masterpiece. But it may have been more than the seeds of literature that captivated him at this time. In 1780, the infamous "black magician" Cagliostro opened a lodge of his Egyptian Rite Freemasonry in Warsaw. Although throughout his life Potocki advocated an inconsistent array of political beliefs, there's strong reason to suspect that he became a Mason in Warsaw then, and that his period in Paris was filled with secret plots to overthrow the monarchy and establish a "universal society" of brotherhood and tolerance. Indeed, scenes and motifs of initiation and secret knowledge run through the *Saragossa Manuscript,* and one of its central figures— the great Sheik of the Gomelez family—is the head of a gigantic scheme that resembles the machinations of the Bavarian Illuminati. Potocki's decision to set his bizarre novel against the wild beauty of the Spanish Sierra Morena may have been influenced by more than the fact that he passed through the area on his way back from Morocco.

In 1788, Potocki returned to Poland, setting up a printing press and publishing company and, a few years later, establishing the first free reading room in Warsaw. In 1790 he made an even greater impression on the Polish capital by becoming one of the first men to ascend in a balloon, floating over the ancient city in the company of the French aeronaut Blanchard, the ubiquitous Osman, and his dog, Lulu. Unable to stay in one place for long, in the late 1790s Potocki found himself on a trek through the Caucasus. Here he learned the secret language of Circassian noblemen and threw himself into the study of the ancient cultures and beliefs of the Slavic people. During this time the count wrote massive volumes on the history, archaeology, and languages of the area with imposing titles like *Principles of Chronology for the Ages Anterior to the Olympiads.* Then, in 1805, in the service of the Russian tsar Alexander I, he was the scientific adviser on an expedition to Peking. At that time China was still resistant to foreign influence and the emperor Yung-Ten turned Potocki back at Ulan Bator in Mongolia.

Unfazed, Potocki absorbed all he could about the customs and culture of the Mongolian people. Given his interest in esoteric matters, one wonders if he came across mention of the fabled underground city of Agarttha, in later years the focus of the eccentric French occultist and orientalist Alexandre Saint-Yves d'Alveydre—as well as that of Potocki's fellow Islamic enthusiast René Guénon. Little is known of Potocki's doings in Mongolia, but it would be surprising if he didn't seek out its more exotic tales and fables. Themes of subterranean mysteries permeate the *Saragossa Manuscript,* with hidden strongholds, buried treasure, and initiatory caves, although these indeed are common tropes in accounts of esotericism. In between ballooning over Warsaw and crossing the Gobi Desert, Potocki found time to turn his hand to literature. One effort, a series of vignettes entitled *Parade*, is a classic of Polish theater. His other classic is, of course, the *Saragossa Manuscript*.

The book has a history as unusual and varied as that of its author. It's believed Potocki began it in 1797 as a series of stories designed to entertain his first wife. It was completed in 1815, just before Potocki took his own life, blowing his brains out with a silver bullet. Legend has it that in his last years Potocki secluded himself in his castle at Uladowka on his Podolia estate. Here he turned melancholy and bored, his health diminished, and his disillusionment grew. The French Revolution had degenerated into a charnel house, and the great dreams of the Illuminati dissolved with the rise of the dictator Napoleon. A scandal surrounding Potocki's divorce from his second wife—in which there were rumors of incest—also took its toll.

Alone, he gave way to morbid fantasies. The thought that he had become a werewolf obsessed him. Potocki is said to have taken the silver knob of a sugar bowl, formed in the shape of a strawberry, and filed this into a bullet, which he had blessed by the castle chaplain. Then, on November 20, 1815 (or, depending on your source, December 2 or 11), he put the bullet in his pistol, stuck the barrel in his mouth, and pulled the trigger, thus earning himself the sobriquet of being "the man who shot himself with a strawberry." In any event, Potocki published the first part of the *Saragossa Manuscript*—comprising the first thirteen days of van Worden's strange adventures—on his own printing press in 1804–05 and distributed it to friends. These, and the following fifty-three days, were written originally in French. Potocki is said to have earned some bad press from the literary establishment of his time for writing and speaking better French than Polish, and to this day there is some controversy over whether the *Saragossa Manuscript* is a work of Polish or French literature.

The second section of the book was published in Paris in 1813 under the title *Avadoro: histoire espagnole* (Avadoro: Spanish history), being made up of tales of a gypsy chief who features in the novel. In 1814, these two separate books were combined into a three-volume edition that appeared in St. Petersburg. After Potocki's death, a Polish translation of the original French appeared in 1847. The original French edition was then lost, and the edition that appeared in Paris in 1989 is basically a translation of the Polish version back into French. A recent English edition is based on this French-Polish version. Although printed editions were for the most part lost throughout the nineteenth century, Potocki's masterpiece was nevertheless easy plunder for writers like Washington Irving and another eccentric litterateur, the mad poet Gérard de Nerval, who was known to stroll the streets of Paris with a lobster on a leash. Irving and Nerval were not alone in stealing copiously from Potocki's fantastic treasure trove in order to meet the nineteenth-century demand for "oriental fictions." This appetite for "Eastern" tales of mystery and magic was sparked in many ways by the work of yet another eccentric writer, William Beckford, builder of the bizarre Gothic folly Fonthill Abbey and author of the decadently exotic novel *Vathek* (1786), which Potocki would certainly have known. Beckford was himself no stranger to the occult world of the Enlightenment, and *Vathek* shares with the *Saragossa Manuscript* a strikingly similar motif: a stairway of fifteen hundred steps. In Beckford's Arabian nightmare, the steps lead upward, to the top of the Tower of the caliph Vathek; in Potocki's they lead down to a cave and the underworld. Beckford's tale of oriental excess and demonic luxury is no more than a rich genius's fantasy of forbidden lust and its willful satisfaction. But for Potocki, the subterranean journey has the resonance of the initiatory rites and magical practices linked to the secret societies he penetrated in prerevolutionary France.

The *Saragossa Manuscript* purports to be a document discovered in 1809 by a French soldier out looting after the fall of the Spanish city of Saragossa to the French and Polish armies. The manuscript recounts the strange adventures of another military officer, Alphonse van Worden, who, some forty years earlier, has come upon a weird crew of ghosts, magicians, dervishes, seductresses, and sheiks as he passes through the mountains of the Sierra Morena on his way to rejoin his regiment in Madrid.

Ignoring warnings of the danger of crossing the mountains alone, Alphonse finds that his troubles begin when he spends the night in a haunted inn. There he encounters two Moorish sisters, Emina and Zubeida, who easily seduce the young man. Enthralled by their charms, he nevertheless hesitates to accept their offer of marriage, since it would mean casting off his Christian beliefs and adopting the word of Islam; he also wonders if they are demons sent to turn him from the true path.

Nevertheless, Alphonse is sufficiently taken with them to drink a potion from a magic cup that produces in him powerful, vivid dreams in which he and the sisters enjoy the delights of the flesh. He is rudely awakened the next morning to find himself, not in the capacious bed of the inn, but in broad daylight, beneath a gallows he had seen the day before, with two bandits hanged upon them. Today, however, the bandits are no longer on the gibbet; they are lying beside him. With disgust, Alphonse realizes that he has spent the night in the embrace of corpses. Thus begins his sixty-six-day sojourn amidst weird and fantastic adventures.

I can only mention some of the many esoteric motifs that appear throughout the tales, as well as the encyclopedic philosophical discourses that accompany them. The gallows suggest the Tarot trump of the Hanged Man, a symbol of spiritual death and initiation; initiation rites and challenges appear in many forms throughout the book. The weird adventures and tales within tales, in which Alphonse is often unsure if he is awake, dreaming, or under the influence of hashish, are a reminder of the ambiguous nature of reality. They also occupy the liminal space between sleep and consciousness, the hypnagogic realm of magic and the paranormal.

Several well-known historical occult figures appear throughout the tales, such as Apollonius of Tyana, Knorr von Rosenroth, and Simon Magus. Several "doublings" also appear, such as the Celestial Twins, suggesting alchemical themes of integration as well as the esoteric notion of the doppelgänger or astral body. Many of the doublings are of a sexual character, suggesting strange erotic practices. The first of these—Alphonse's encounter with Emina and Zubeida, whom he first meets in a cellar—suggests the uncertain terrain the reader is about to enter. These delightful but dangerous twins are "subterraneans," creatures of the underworld. They are also devotees of a strange, foreign faith.

As the scholar Joscelyn Godwin points out in *The Theosophical Enlightenment*, "The initiatic journey to Islamic soil has been a repeated theme of European esotericism, ever since the Templars settled in Jerusalem and Christian Rosenkreuz learnt his trade in Damascus." What troubles the young Alphonse about his new girlfriends, aside from the fact that they may really be the ghosts of two bandits, is their enticements to abandon his Christian beliefs and adopt Islam, a horror that Potocki, with his obsession with all things Arabic, obviously didn't share.

For adventurous Europeans of the nineteenth century, the East represented all that went beyond the staid morality of Christianity. Yet, if all Potocki wanted was to add another oriental fiction to the proliferation of Eastern tales that sprang up after Antoine Galland produced his French translation of *The Arabian Nights* in 1717, why would he set his phantasmagoric novel in Spain, an exceedingly Catholic country? The answer, I think, lies in Potocki's possible involvement with the Bavarian Illuminati and the mystico-political intrigues of prerevolutionary France.

The secret society known as the Bavarian Illuminati began on May 1, 1776, the brainchild of one Adam Weishaupt, a professor of canonical law at Ingoldstat University in Bavaria. Weishaupt, drunk with the elixir of rationalism, had a vision of a free, egalitarian Europe, rid of the tyranny of the monarchies. To achieve this end, he became a Freemason in order to use the lodges' vast network of contacts and hierarchies. Quickly his disciples infiltrated most other lodges; even Cagliostro, it is said, was an early convert. Cagliostro, we know, opened a lodge of his Egyptian Rite Freemasonry in Warsaw in 1780. The Illuminati's aim was to gain members among the rich and powerful of society, targeting aristocrats and noblemen of reformist views. I have suggested that Potocki may have been initiated into Masonry in Cagliostro's Warsaw lodge. If so, and if Cagliostro was indeed a member of the Illuminati, then Potocki would be exactly the kind of individual they would bring into their circle. The fact that Weishaupt claimed that Mohammed himself was an initiate of the society would certainly have piqued the young count's interest.

The themes of esoteric and political intrigue running through the *Saragossa Manuscript* have clear parallels with the aims of the Illuminati, but there are other links that strengthen the case for it being an Illuminist work. One is Potocki's love of things Islamic. In the 1500s, in the mountains of Afghanistan, an earlier "Illuminati" rose up: the Roshaniya, or "Illuminated Ones." With his passion for orientalism and arcane knowledge, Potocki might possibly have known of this cult. Led by "the sage of Illumination," Bayezid Ansari, the Illuminated Ones claimed to be descendants of the "helpers of Mohammed" after his flight from Mecca. According to some authorities, references exist that link this cult to a "House of Wisdom" in Cairo, which existed in the eleventh century. Mention of a House of Wisdom links Roshaniya to another Islamic secret society, the Assassins, who also spoke of a "House of Science" located in Cairo. The Assassins' reign of terror also began in the last years of the eleventh century.

Archetypal mystical-political intriguers, the Assassins set the tone for the conspiracy theories that gathered around the Freemasons in the nineteenth century. In his *Geschichte der Assassinen* (History of the Assassins, 1818), Joseph von Hammer-Purgstall wrote: "As in the West, revolutionary societies arose from the bosom of the Freemasons, so in the East did the Assassins spring from the Ismaili sect." Bayezid Ansari was said to have been inspired to create the Roshaniya by a meeting with an Ismaili missionary. Like the Assassins and Illuminati, the Roshaniya aimed at gaining political control by subverting the status quo; they also practiced a form of meditation known as *khilwat*, or silence, an exercise said to stimulate supernatural abilities. Bayezid exercised absolute control over his followers, as did the Assassins' Old Man of the Mountain and Potocki's Great Sheik of the Gomelez. Preaching a doctrine similar to that famously attributed to the leader of the Assassins, Hassan ibn Saba—"Nothing is true, everything is permitted"—Bayezid was able to achieve considerable political power, with disciples and followers willing to commit all manner of crimes, including murder. As in Weishaupt's Illuminati, women were employed by Bayezid as agents, their powers of seduction deemed to be often more powerful means of persuasion than rational argument; *The Saragossa Manuscript* echoes this idea in Alphonse's initiation by the Moorish sisters. Eventually, Bayezid Ansari and Roshaniya were suppressed by the Moguls.

Yet another pre-Weishaupt version of the Illuminati flourished in Spain. In 1512 the sect of the Alumbrados, or "Illuminated Ones," began in Guadalajara. It rose among the circles of Franciscan friars responsible for some of the first great works of mysticism to be published in Spain. The cult's basic belief was in an "illumination by the Holy Spirit," a kind of gnosis that did away with the need for priest or church. Soon detected by the Spanish Inquisition, the cult existed in different forms until it was finally suppressed in 1623. Oddly enough, this same year saw strange notices announcing the arrival of yet another secret society, the Rosicrucians, in Paris. This may be more than a coincidence given the similarities among the practices of the Rosicrucians, the Alumbrados, and certain Sufi sects; for example, the Alumbrados practiced a kind of intense mental concentration, similar to the *khilwat* of the Roshaniya, which they called "mental prayer."

Although a Christian cult, the Alumbrados shared some of the erotic practices of the Illuminati and Roshaniya, as well as the Moorish sisters. When the church finally crushed them, the Alumbrados were, like the Templars (also linked to the Illuminati), accused of sexual perversion. The cult was made up of priests and priestesses and combined a form of free love with dramatic displays of mystical intoxication. Members were encouraged to induce ecstasies and trances and, like the Great Sheik of the Gomelez, leaders of the Alumbrados demanded absolute obedience. In return they absolved their followers of all responsibility to secular and spiritual authorities. During the Inquisition's trials, it turned out that many of the sect's members were *conversos*, or New Christians, descendants of Jews converted to Christianity after the pogroms of 1391. Judaism, like Islam, attracted Potocki as an exotic alternative to the Christianity of his time, and the Spanish Jews were of course responsible for the great system of mystical and magical thought known as Kabbalah, notions of which run throughout the *Saragossa Manuscript*.

Rosicrucian symbolism also abounds in Potocki's masterpiece, most clearly in the scene in which Alphonse finds himself in a cave illuminated by many lamps. There he discovers a massive vein of gold and the tools necessary to extract the precious metal. In the *Fama fraternitatis* (Rumor of the Brotherhood) of 1614—one of the earliest Rosicrucian tracts—the authors promise anyone coming forth to join the society "more gold than both the Indies bring to the king of Spain." Each day in the cave, Alphonse extracts a quantity of the metal equal to his weight. In Rosicrucian legend, Christian Rosenkreuz, the mythical founder of the society, was buried in 1484, in a hidden tomb, after dying at the age of 106. In 1604, this tomb was said to have been discovered and, inside, his uncorrupted body lay in a seven-sided vault, lit by a powerful lamp. The Rosicrucians were Hermeticists, Kabbalists, and alchemists, but they shunned the vulgar idea of alchemy as a means of making material gold. The gold they sought was spiritual; clearly the gold that Alphonse mines is of a similar nature.

In setting his nineteenth-century "illuminated" tale in Spain, the European land that for a time fell to the followers of the Prophet, Potocki, whose incredible erudition may well have uncovered Weishaupt's predecessors, forged his own bonds with the earlier Illuminists. In any event, *A Manuscript Found in Saragossa* displays the best virtues of the mystical Enlightenment: tolerance, curiosity, and a lively interest in the beliefs and practices of cultures outside the Christocentric Europe of the time. If, in his last days, the man who shot himself with a strawberry succumbed to melancholy and despair, he nevertheless left us a manuscript full of wonder and magic.

Éliphas Lévi: The Professor of Transcendental Magic

Accordding to most accounts, modern occultism was invented by Alphonse Louis Constant, who was born in Paris in 1810 and who wrote his books under the pseudonym Éliphas Lévi, supposedly the Hebrew equivalent of his birth name. At that time an atmosphere of the East clung to Jews, an exotic flavor of distant lands, strange practices, and magical lore, which appealed to Constant. His writing is full of portentous references to the secret mysteries of the Talmud, the *Zohar*, and other Hebrew texts. He was also a passionate, if unreliable, devotee of Kabbalah. Having a Hebrew name was undoubtedly good for his credibility as a Kabbalistic savant.

The son of a shoemaker, Constant grew up in humble surroundings near the Boulevard Saint Germain. Although he was dreamy and solitary, his quick mind impressed the parish priest, who helped to get Alphonse sent to the "little seminary" of Saint Nicolas du Chardonnet and from there to the seminary of Saint Sulpice. Here he studied for the priesthood until, as the story goes, he was eventually relieved of the cloth for "preaching doctrines contrary to the church."

Exactly what those doctrines were is unclear, but it is very likely they had to do with sex. His doubt about the priesthood came in the form of a young girl he tutored for her first Holy Communion. The girl's poor mother begged Constant to instruct her, saying that a man of his kindness couldn't refuse. In the girl's beautiful blue eyes he discovered the overwhelming need for human love—although he assures us the inspiration was not carnal. Suddenly, the idea of a life of cold renunciation repelled him, and he abandoned the priesthood just before taking his final vows.

After leaving Saint Sulpice, Constant earned his crust acting with a touring theatrical group. He was a talented artist and provided illustrations for a magazine called *Beautiful Women of Paris and the Provinces*. His drawings appear in his own books as well as others, including an edition of Alexandre Dumas's novel *The Count of Monte Cristo*. He wrote several pamphlets of a radical socialist nature—more rhetorical than well argued—and supported himself as best he could on the periphery of the Parisian literary world.

In 1839, Constant met Alphonse Esquiros, author of a strange work of "high fantasy," *The Magician*. It embodied, Lévi tells us, "all that the romanticism of the period conceived to be most bizarre." This included a harem of dead ladies, a bronze automaton that preached chastity, and a hermaphrodite who was in love with the moon.

Esquiros invited Constant to visit a visionary prophet, "The Mapah," an old man called Simon Ganneau, who was involved in a strange royalist messianic intrigue. Ganneau had the peculiar habit of wearing a woman's cloak while he spoke to his disciples of the creation of the universe, the fall of man, and other occult revelations. Although he had originally gone to scoff, Lévi was impressed by the weird scene in the Mapah's squalid attic.

In his *Histoire de la magie* (History of magic, 1860) Lévi describes Ganneau as "a bearded man of majestic demeanor . . . surrounded by several men, bearded and ecstatic like himself." The woman's cloak gave the prophet the "air of a destitute dervish," and a white froth would gather on his lips when he warmed to his subject. Ganneau's wife—motionless, "like an entranced somnambulist"—believed herself to be the reincarnation of Marie Antoinette. Not to be outdone, Ganneau claimed to be Louis XVII. Esquiros and Constant forgot their laughter and, taken with Ganneau's message to give "the last word of revolution and to seal the abyss of anarchy," they duly joined the converted.

One of the Mapah's disciples started the revolution of 1848, at least according to Lévi. This intense young man, named Sobrier, who "believed himself predestined to save the world by provoking the supreme crisis of universal revolution," began shouting on the streets of Paris. Accompanied by two "street arabs"—one with a torch, the other beating time—he went through the streets with half of Paris behind him. The mob stopped before the Hôtel des Capucines; a shot was fired and the riot broke out. If this story is true, esotericism in the nineteenth century had more of an effect on the exoteric world than is usually suspected.

Constant himself was imprisoned for eight months for writing a socialist tract called *The Gospel of Liberty* (1839). His personal life had its disappointments, too. In Evreux, he had seduced an assistant headmistress, who bore him an illegitimate child. The one glaring misdeed in a life otherwise devoted to social utopianism and mystical absorption occurred when Constant abandoned the teacher and became infatuated with her student, Noémie Cadiot. In 1846, at the age of thirty-six, Constant married Noémie, then seventeen years old. They had a daughter who died in childhood, and soon after the death, Noémie left him. Lévi was devastated, but Noémie's desertion proved the catalyst that transformed the socialist dreamer into Éliphas Lévi, master of the mystic arts.

In 1852, the year before Noémie's desertion, Constant came under the influence of one of the most curious figures of the nineteenth century, the eccentric Polish émigré Józef Maria Hoene-Wronski. A soldier in the Polish and Russian armies, Hoene-Wronski studied at the observatory at Marseille between 1803 and 1810. There he developed a fantastically complex theory of the origin and structure of the universe. Communicating with the major astronomers and physicists of the time, Hoene-Wronski's happy years in Marseille ended when he published the results of his research. These were so controversial that the faculty of the Institute of Marseille forced him to leave the observatory, and intellectual persecution dogged him for the rest of his life.

Absolutely committed, in the face of scorn, ridicule, and abject poverty, to his vision of universal and fundamental knowledge, Hoene-Wronski ignited the latent occultist in Constant. Hoene-Wronski's Pythagorean theories held numbers to be the key to the mysteries of the universe. He was also preoccupied with a perpetual motion machine, "squaring the circle," and an invention he called the *prognomètre*, a machine designed to make predictions.

But it was Hoene-Wronski's *messianisme*—the name he gave to his synthesis of philosophy, religion, science, and politics—that truly inspired Constant. Charged with a new mission, Constant plunged into writing his first magical treatise, *Dogme de la haute magie* (Dogma of high magic, 1854). This, along with its second part, *Rituel de la haute magie* (Ritual of high magic, 1856), was ponderously translated into English by the British occultist A. E. Waite as *Transcendental Magic* (1896).

It was while writing this that Constant's wife left him. Constant contributed to a leftist paper, the *Revue progressive*, owned by the Marquis de Montferrier; through this association, the Marquis became interested in the talented and beautiful Noémie. At first he invited her to write for the paper as well—which she did under the name of Claude Vignon—but she soon became his mistress. Immersed in his Kabbalistic studies, Constant did not notice what was going on until it was too late.

Devastated by his wife's desertion, Constant lost himself in his studies. It was like some terrible initiation. When the *Dogme* appeared on the bookstalls of Paris, it was a sign that Alphonse, the social theorist and ex-abbé, was no more. The title page proclaimed his new identity, Éliphas Lévi. Thereafter he was known to his students and across Europe as the Professor of Transcendental Magic. The book's opening was guaranteed to hook its readers. "Behind the veil of all hieratic and mystical allegories of ancient doctrines," Lévi wrote, "behind the darkness and strange ordeals of all initiations, under the seal of all sacred writings, in the ruins of Nineveh or Thebes, on the crumbling stones of old temples and on the blackened visage of the Assyrian or Egyptian sphinx, in the monstrous or marvelous paintings which interpret to the faithful of India the inspired pages of the Vedas, in the cryptic emblems of our old books on alchemy, in the ceremonies practiced at reception by all secret societies, there are found indications of a doctrine which is everywhere the same and everywhere concealed."

As Colin Wilson remarks in *The Occult,* for all its sonorous power, what Lévi claims here is untrue. There is no single "secret doctrine" behind the various forms of occultism and mystical lore throughout history. Yet Lévi's desire to see one is in keeping with the early nineteenth-century fascination with discovering the "roots" of things, natural and social. Discovering the sources of the Nile, of mythology, and of language—not to mention the origin of the species—occupied the best minds of the century. Freud's attempt to root neurosis and dreams in sexuality can be seen as the last major undertaking of this sort.

But more important than Lévi's erroneous belief in a primal ur-doctrine of magic is the expectation that this stirring if overly romantic passage creates. It suggests that behind the everyday world, behind the history written in textbooks and the "current events" found in newspapers, lies another world, one of deeper and more powerful meaning. This is one of the central themes that Lévi bequeathed to the occultists who have followed him.

Just decades later, the same motif can be seen in the writings of Madame Blavatsky and her tales of mystic Mahatmas who direct the evolution of mankind from secret places in the Himalayas; in G. I. Gurdjieff's stories of hidden sanctuaries in Central Asia; and, later, in the tales of lost knowledge and vanished civilizations in the fictions of H. P. Lovecraft.

In 1853, after his wife's desertion, the born-again magician packed a bag and set out for London, staying at a hotel in Bloomsbury. He carried letters of introduction to some of the most influential English occultists; as his career as a mage had scarcely begun, his reputation can hardly account for this. More than a century before the Internet, it seems, devotees of eccentric interests were already networking across considerable distances. It also implies that a formidable international occult cabal was well established in nineteenth-century Europe.

One of these contacts was Sir Edward Bulwer-Lytton (later Lord Lytton). Bulwer-Lytton was one of England's most successful novelists, having already published works like *The Last Days of Pompeii*. Several occult novels—*Zanoni, A Strange Story*, and *Vril: The Power of the Coming Race*—are notable for their suffusion of occult lore and esoteric wisdom. The two got on well, inaugurating a deep and mutually influential friendship.

But by far the most important event of Lévi's London visit was his famous invocation of the ghost of Apollonius of Tyana, one of the greatest magicians of antiquity. Lévi's account reads like something out of a supernatural thriller. The ceremony, commissioned by a mysterious woman in black, took three weeks to prepare and is described in his *Rituel de la haute magie* (Ritual of high magic, 1856). Apparently, the giant figure that appeared before the altar did not look how Lévi imagined Apollonius would. Lévi fainted, and his right arm, touched by the phantom, was numb for days after.

"Am I to conclude from this that I really evoked, saw, and touched the great of Apollonius of Tyana?" Lévi asks. Unwilling or unable to explain the "physical laws" by which this could happen, Lévi nevertheless maintained that he did see and did touch the apparition, "clearly and distinctly, apart from dreaming, and that this is sufficient to establish the real efficacy of magical ceremonies."

Lévi's reputation as a true mage flourished, and other volumes followed, including *La clef des grands mystères* (The key of the great mysteries, 1861). The "esotourists" and occult travelers that visited him in his Paris apartments were usually greeted by a rotund man of red complexion, medium height, small, piercing eyes, prodigious bald cranium, full black beard and moustache, wrapped in his ubiquitous monk's robe. The rooms themselves were jammed with occult bric-a-brac. On an altar covered in sumptuous drapery and gilt vessels sat a Hebrew roll of the Law. Above this hung a golden triangle with the ineffable Tetragrammaton (YHVH, the Hebrew name of God) emblazoned on it. Talismans, skulls, and his magical apparatus jostled for space in his small chambers with a life-size painting of a woman representing Holy Kabbalah and with Hoene-Wronski's prognomètre. The atmosphere was at once priestly and theatrical.

Lévi's fame as a master of the occult mysteries brought him a clutch of eager and supportive students. When the Englishman Kenneth Mackenzie—alleged adept and member of the Societas Rosicruciana in Anglia—visited, Lévi greeted him wearing a felt hat which, Lévi said, he was compelled to wear owing to "an affliction of the head." In the course of a conversation on the Tarot, Mackenzie noticed a figurine of the Egyptian goddess Isis. He remarked to Lévi that it was an especially fine piece of work; Lévi replied that the item was quite ordinary in Paris, being a very large tobacco jar.

Lévi's students included two Polish noblemen, Counts Alexander Braszynsky and Georges de Mniszech, as well as another Pole, named Nowakowski, who worked as a doctor in Berlin, and who was drawn to the occult through a fascination with the dervishes. But Lévi's closest disciple was an Italian nobleman, Baron Nicolas-Joseph Spedalieri; Lévi's letters to him fill nine volumes.

France's humiliating defeat in the Franco-Prussian War of 1870–71 brought Lévi misery. Not only had Lévi nourished high hopes for France as the savior of civilization, but the siege of Paris made his life very difficult. The Commune that followed was no better received by Lévi, who in his last years had lost much of his revolutionary fire.

Toward the end, his days were painful; the headaches and dizzy spells increased; he suffered from dropsy and gangrenous feet, and he spent long, sleepless nights in his armchair. Stoical, Lévi faced the approach of the Great Unknown with courage, surrounded by friends and helpers.

At two o'clock in the afternoon of May 3, 1875, Éliphas Lévi, once described as "the last of the magi," passed from his armchair in the Rue de Sèvres into the *Ain Soph,* the unmanifest Limitless Light of the

Kabbalists. He left his manuscripts, books, and scientific instruments, including his prognomètre, to his disciple de Mniszech.

The year of his death is worth noting, for it was one predicted for him. In a letter to Baron Spedalieri, dated 1865, Lévi told of a memorable visit by a curious character, one Juliano Capella. Although the two had never met, Capella told Lévi: "I know your entire life, past, present, and future. It is regulated by the inexorable law of numbers," a claim that echoed the insights of Hoene-Wronski. "You are a man of the pentagram," Lévi's uninvited guest continued, "and the years marked by the number five are always fateful ones for you." Capella then announced that 1875 would mark "the natural end" of Lévi's life.

One wonders if the Professor of Transcendental Magic ever employed his prognomètre to corroborate this unfortunately accurate prediction.

CHAPTER FIVE

The Alchemy of
August Strindberg

In 1894, after years of painful struggle and almost universal rejection by his countrymen, the Swedish playwright August Strindberg suffered a spiritual collapse, an emotional breakdown that left him incapable of creative work. That Strindberg had reached a dead end isn't surprising. Vilified in his homeland for naturalistic works like *Miss Julie* and *The Father*, he had already been through two divorces—a third was yet to come—as well as many years of impoverishment and the loss of his three children from his first marriage. His second marriage, to the Austrian journalist Frida Uhl, had just ended bitterly. This meant estrangement from yet another child and the loss of Frida's considerable dowry. At forty-five, penniless and alone, it's unsurprising that Strindberg questioned the point of going on. Yet he was a man who possessed demonic persistence, and the route out of his impasse led through one of the strangest episodes in the turbulent life of a master of modern literature.

After his failure in Sweden and a stint in Berlin, Strindberg looked to Paris for a last assault on fame. Paris was the cultural capital of the nineteenth century, and by 1893, some of Strindberg's works had already been performed there. But it wasn't just literary glory that attracted him. Like London, St. Petersburg, and other European capitals, the Paris of the fin de siècle had been bitten by the occultism bug. Ever since 1856, when Éliphas Lévi invented modern occultism with the publication of *Dogme et rituel de la haute magie* (Dogma and ritual of high magic),

Paris had been a haven for the esoterically inclined. Although a founder of naturalism, Strindberg had a deep interest in magic, mysticism, and other forms of the occult. He was also fascinated by science, considering himself equal to its professionals. In 1893 he published his first work of speculative natural history, *Antibarbarus* (Antibarbarian), a work that pitted the man of genius against the academic plodders, arguing that the poet's eye saw more deeply that the professor's methodical squint.

When it came to the occult, Strindberg's pet practice was alchemy. According to one account, by 1894 there were an estimated 50,000 alchemists in Paris. Whether this is an exaggeration or not, in the last years of the nineteenth century, Paris was undoubtedly a place where occultism mixed with the avant-garde. In 1891, J.-K. Huysmans, onetime follower of Émile Zola and author of the decadent classic *À rebours* (Against nature), had shocked the literary public with his graphic depiction of a Black Mass in his satanic novel *Là-Bas* (Down there). Huysmans's involvement with the Parisian occult underground popularized what was already a well-tenanted demimonde; it also fueled a growing fad for returning to the safe embrace of the church after a titillating walk on the dark side. After finding himself in the middle of an occult feud between the notorious Abbé Boullan and the self-styled Rosicrucian Joséphin Sar Péladan, full of astral attacks and, as Huysmans called them, "fluidic fisticuffs," the man who kicked off the Yellow Decade ended his days at a Benedictine monastery.

Such Rosicrucian roistering wasn't unusual. A few years before, the decadent poet Stanislas de Guaita, a devotee of Baudelaire, morphine addict (he would die of an overdose in 1897), and onetime student of Sar Péladan fought an extended battle with his ex-master. Most of the fighting took place in print, but the recognition that magical warfare was not uncommon in fin de siècle Paris adds a depth to Strindberg's uncanny adventures, one that commentators sometimes miss. Undoubtedly, between 1894 and 1896, Strindberg came close to, and probably did experience, a schizoid episode. But it is just possible that the weird experiences he recounts in his obsessive record *Inferno*—based, in part, on his even more bizarre *Occult Diary*—did not solely originate in a great mind's pitiable crackup. Without doubt, the ingredients for a complete mental breakdown are there: intense stress, loneliness, poverty, and an uncertain future, abetted in no small part by Strindberg's devotion to a popular magical elixir of the day, absinthe. But the strange events that make up Strindberg's *Inferno* are precisely the sort that fueled one of the burning questions of the age: the thin line between genius and madness. A line that, by all accounts, Strindberg passed over frequently.

Throughout his career, Strindberg had periodic bouts of revulsion against literature. His artistic credo practically ensured this. "I regard it as my dreadful duty to be truthful," he wrote, "and life is indescribably ugly." Such sentiments prompted his plunge into alchemy. It may seem strange that, considering himself a scientist, Strindberg chose alchemy as his path to immortality. But his approach to science was anything but orthodox. His aim in *Antibarbarus* was to "explain" the nature of sulfur, the transmutation of carbon and other elements, and the composition of water and air. Claiming to be a "transformist" like Darwin and a monist like the German naturalist Ernst Haeckel, Strindberg declared: "I have committed myself to the assumption that all elements and all forces are related. And *if* they derive from one source, then they sprang into existence by means of condensation and attenuation, of copulating and crossbreeding, of heredity and transformation . . . and whatever else one cares to suggest."

This cavalier attitude didn't win the critics' approval. When the book appeared, Strindberg's pretentions to science were dismissed as a sign of monomania, its author lambasted for his lack of logic and incapacity for experiment. But for the alchemist, transformation is the key, and Strindberg's speculative approach is in the great magical tradition. Writing to his young botanist friend, Bengt Lindforss, Strindberg said: "I doubt all experiments. . . . I believe rather in the depth of my conscious thought, or more correctly, my unconscious thought." His method was to put himself "into a state of unconsciousness, not with drink, but by distractions, games, cards, sleep, novels, without bothering about results or acceptability, and something emerges that I can believe in."

Weird as it seems, Strindberg's "science" was right in line with the latest developments in art. Before his descent on Paris, he had published an essay, "The New Arts, or the Role of Chance in Artistic Creation." This, along with another article on "Deranged Sense Impressions," deals with the curious power of the mind to alter its perceptions—in a word, to "recreate" reality. Like many other artists and poets, Strindberg rebelled against the neat, orderly, "objective" universe being revealed by an increasingly triumphant rationalist science. In its place, he argued for a world open to strange forces, and the influence of consciousness itself, a position made commonplace decades later with the rise of quantum physics. In "The New Arts" he describes the "oscillations of his sense impressions" and recounts how, seen from a certain angle, a cow becomes two peasants embracing each other, then a tree trunk, and then something else, and how the figures at a picnic are really a plowman's coat and knapsack thrown over his cart. Strindberg would later describe his own method of writing as something like a trance state. It begins, he said, "with fermentation or some sort of agreeable fever which passes into ecstasy or intoxication." His considerable absinthe intake surely had a hand in this. Nevertheless, by the next century, with Dada and Surrealism, the notion that reality is plastic, and that consciousness and chance affect what we experience, would become standard components of aesthetic theory.

But Strindberg was interested in more than a new approach to art. He took his alchemy seriously and, soon after his arrival in Paris, turned his back on the literary world and got to work on the archetypal alchemical project: making gold.

His first step was to obtain experimental proof of his ideas about transformation. He set out to prove the presence of carbon in sulfur. "Back once more in my miserable student's room," he writes, "I delved into my trunk and drew forth from their hiding place six crucibles of fine porcelain which I robbed myself to buy. A pair of tongs and a packet of pure sulfur completed the apparatus of my laboratory. All that remained was to make a fire of furnace heat in the stove."

He did. The flame from his makeshift furnace was so great that he soon suffered appalling burns, the skin on his hands "peeling off in scales." After more experiments, the burns worsened, and his chapped, cracked hands, irritated by coke dust, oozed blood. The pain was intolerable, yet, convinced of his success, Strindberg continued. The next step was to show the presence of hydrogen and oxygen. But his apparatus was inadequate and his funds were dwindling. Destitute and in agony, Strindberg had reached another dead end. When the veins in his arms started to swell from blood poisoning, friends collected money and put him in the Hôpital de Saint-Louis.

There Strindberg made friends with a pharmacist who took an interest in his pursuits and allowed him to work in his laboratory. Urged on, he sent the results of his experiments to a firm of chemists to be analyzed. Their tests proved positive: the sulfur he submitted did indeed contain carbon. More encouragement followed. A summary of Strindberg's scientific work appeared in *Le petit temps*, followed by long articles on "Strindberg the scientist" in the highly respected periodical *La science française* and the widely read *Le Figaro*. On the strength of these, Strindberg petitioned to conduct further experiments using the laboratory at the Sorbonne. Although the faculty thought little of his work, he was granted permission, and he carried out his tests. Further signs of success appeared. An engineer at a chemical factory in Rouen who read of his experiments wrote to him saying that they threw light on "hitherto unexplained phenomena in the manufacture of sulfuric acid and sulfides." At the same time, a correspondence with the distinguished chemist Marcellin Berthelot suggested to Strindberg that he was on the right track.

Soon Strindberg believed he had succeeded in extracting gold from iron. It was around this time that he came into contact with the Parisian alchemical underground. A young man named François Jollivet-Castelot, the author of *La vie et l'âme de la matière* (The life and soul of matter), which Strindberg had read with enthusiasm, had heard of Strindberg's work and approached him, convinced the great playwright had actually succeeded in the alchemical dream. Jollivet-Castelot later became the editor of an alchemical journal, *L'hyperchimie*, and published Strindberg's account of his alchemical work "The Synthesis of Gold." A rising star in the alchemical subculture, Strindberg's celebrity was assured when Gérard Encausse, better known under his occult pseudonym Papus, published an account of his work in the periodical *L'initiation*. "August Strindberg," Papus wrote, "who combines vast knowledge with his great talent as a writer, has just achieved a synthesis of gold from iron." His work, Papus continued, "confirms all the assertions of the alchemists."

This was high praise. The author of several influential works, as leader of the Groupe Indépendant d'Études Esoteriques and Grand Master of the Martinist order, Papus was a powerful figure in the Parisian occult underground. He was also indirectly involved in the magical feud between Huysmans, Sar Péladan, and de Guaita. When Papus elected Strindberg an honorary master of La Société Alchimique de France, it's understandable the accolade went to his head. After years of obscurity, rejection, and accusations of madness, to be accepted as a genius by men whose intelligence he respected must have given him some satisfaction.

Yet his alchemical adventure wasn't purely benign. Nurtured by his occult obsessions, his "deranged sense impressions" began to get out of hand. At first he chalked his weird perceptual mutations up to chance and the vagaries of his unconscious, but increasingly he recognized in them the hands of an occult intelligence he called "the Powers" and "the Unseen." The world these occult forces led him through soon turned into a kind of waking dream—or nightmare.

On a walk to the Luxembourg Gardens he spied his initials, A. S., painted on a shop window, rising out of a silver-white cloud, surmounted by a rainbow. He took this as a positive omen. At a stall on the Boulevard Saint Michel, "by chance" he picked up an old chemistry text by the Franco-Spanish toxicologist Mateo Orfila. Opening it at random, he hit on a passage that confirmed his alchemical intuition. "Sulfur has been included among the elements," Orfila wrote, and certain experiments "seem to prove that it contains hydrogen and oxygen." Later, during a walk in the Montparnasse Cemetery after his experiments at the Sorbonne, "chance" drew Strindberg to Orfila's grave, which he didn't know was there, and a later walk down the Rue d'Assas found him oddly drawn to a monastery-like building. It turned out to be the Hotel Orfila. Strindberg soon settled in for a short stay in purgatory.

Never easy on himself, Strindberg felt he was being tested. He talked to "the Powers," thanked them, and asked them advice. He saw their work everywhere. Money appeared miraculously, allowing him to buy instruments. Observing the embryo of a walnut under a microscope, Strindberg was convinced that he could see two tiny hands, clasped in prayer, emerging from the seed. Another sign. On a "chance" trip to the country, a stone was transformed into a statue of a Roman knight. Pleased with this effect, he looked in the direction in which the "statue" was pointing. On a wall he saw the initials F and S. He first thought of his second wife, Frida Strindberg. But then he realized that it was really the chemical symbols for iron and sulfur (Fe and S), the ingredients, he believed, for alchemical gold (but also for iron pyrites, or fool's gold). The weirdness continued. A crumpled pillow became a Michelangelo bust, then a likeness of the devil. A shadow in his room became a statue of Zeus. He had precognitive dreams. A dead friend appeared, offering a large American coin. When Strindberg reached for it, the friend disappeared. The next morning he received a letter from America. Arriving months late, it informed him of an offer of twelve thousand francs to write something for the Chicago Exhibition. But the deadline had passed, and the money, a fortune for Strindberg, was lost.

A host of strange simulacra followed. In a zinc bath that he used for making gold by the "wet method," he saw a remarkable "landscape." There were "small hills covered with conifers . . . plains, with orchards and cornfields . . . a river . . . the ruins of a castle," all formed by the evaporation of salts of iron. It was only a month later, during a visit to his daughter, whom he hadn't seen for two years, that he recognized his vision as the landscape around his mother-in-law's house. Making gold by the "dry method" produced its own terrors. Destitute once again, Strindberg felt he had to succeed. But "the Powers" had decreed otherwise. After melting borax in terrific heat, all he found was a skull with two glistening eyes. On another occasion a chunk of charred coal revealed a bizarre formation: a body with a rooster's head, a human trunk, and distorted limbs. It looked, he remarked, "like one of the demons that used to perform in the witches' Sabbaths of the Middle Ages." Later discoveries included two gnomes in billowing garments embracing each other, and a Madonna and Child, done up in Byzantine style.

A reading of Swedenborg convinced Strindberg that his alchemical experiments were unholy and that for his "salvation," "the Powers" had consigned him to hell. His torments took the form of various magical attacks. Strindberg was undoubtedly highly strung and thin-skinned, and some of his "tortures"—such as finding that his hotel room window opened on the toilets of the neighboring building—smack more of inconvenience and discomfort than anything else. But some are more in line with the magical goings-on familiar to the time. Strindberg began to feel there was an occult conspiracy against him. Letters he discovered in the Hotel Orfila convinced him someone was spying on his alchemical activities. The sound of pianos playing eerie, disturbing music followed him everywhere. He was convinced that the Polish decadent writer Stanislaw Przybyszewski had come from Berlin to kill him.

Something like a persecution complex developed. His "supersensitive nerves" detected strange subterranean vibrations. The idea that he was the target of evil emanations obsessed him. Baffling "coincidences" appeared everywhere. Mysterious noises from the rooms next door tormented him, and he was convinced that someone was trying to kill him using an "electrical machine." He walked around Paris in a state of tense expectancy, awaiting "an eruption, an earthquake, or thunderbolt." Friends and acquaintances now became demons, sent by "the Powers" to show him the error of his ways, and each night he suffered anxiety attacks in which he endured the recurrent onslaughts of his torturers. For some time, because he had rejected the teachings of Madame Blavatsky, he was convinced his assailants were a group of Theosophists. As with his numerous simulacra, once the restraints of reason were lifted—"I no longer try to find a motive for my actions. I act extempore"—he saw signs of his persecution everywhere.

Eventually, through Swedenborg's philosophy, Strindberg passed through his ordeal, convinced that "the Powers" had put him through the mill in order to aid his spiritual evolution. By 1897, his interest in alchemy abated, and the urge to write had returned, one product of which was *Inferno*. In 1898 he began work on *To Damascus*, perhaps his greatest play. His belief in "the Powers" remained for the rest of his life.

It's possible that Strindberg's taste for absinthe was the real reason for his strange experiences. As consumed in his day, absinthe contained oil of thuja, a powerful and addictive hallucinogen. Habitual use resulted in anxiety, fear, hallucinations, a sense of paralysis and paranoia—all symptoms clearly experienced by Strindberg. And yet his occult episodes included periods when he apparently went without drink. So what happened?

Strindberg was an enormously creative individual, with incredible powers of imagination, a terrific will, and an ability to withstand blows that would destroy most people. Like many other creative individuals, he at times gained access to hitherto unknown potentials—hidden powers. Yet, for a variety of reasons, he was also plagued by a paralyzing sense of guilt. My own belief is that, dammed up as they were by his perpetual self-revulsion, Strindberg's creative energies emerged in other ways—some paranormal, some simply mad—and the "persecution" he endured was the work of his own unconscious, rebelling against the abandonment of his real task. As he himself wrote, "In the great crises of life, when existence itself is threatened, the soul attains transcendent powers."

This is not to say that Strindberg's alchemical experiences were worthless but rather that they were a distraction from his real work. I'm inclined to think Strindberg himself knew this. Without the artist's hand to guide them, Strindberg's "deranged sense impressions" became eerie, oppressive fantasies aided, if not actually created, by a powerful intoxicant. "The Powers," however, knew better, and the "unseen hand"—Strindberg's own—showed him the error of his ways.

CHAPTER SIX

The Inimitable Madame B.

New York's East Side isn't somewhere that we'd usually associate with the start of a new spiritual movement, but on September 13, 1875, that's exactly what it was. In a room cluttered with oriental bric-a-brac above an often dangerous neighborhood, three people came together on that day to form an occult society that would have a profound influence, not only on modern spirituality and esotericism, but on practically the whole of modern culture. Two of the three were men with distinguished careers behind them. William Quan Judge, an Irish immigrant, had worked his way up from poor beginnings to become a lawyer and had only a few years earlier passed the New York Bar exam at the age of twenty-one. The forty-two-year-old Colonel Henry Steel Olcott was an officer in the Civil War, a journalist, and an agriculturalist, and had been a member of the commission that investigated Abraham Lincoln's assassination.

But it was the third, female member of this triumvirate that was the real center of attraction. Even before landing on US soil, which she did in 1873, she had lived a life packed with enough adventures to last several incarnations. Revolutionary, spiritualist, music teacher, cousin to a future Russian prime minister, Sergei Witte (a friend of the "Holy Devil," Gregory Rasputin), and granddaughter of a princess—to name only a few of her many distinctions—in a century noted for larger than life characters, Olcott and Judge's partner was perhaps the most supersized of them all, both literally and metaphorically. I'm surprised no one has yet made a film of her life, although in today's world of anorexic supermodels, finding an actress willing to play a 232-pound leading lady might be difficult.

Madame Helena Petrovna Blavatsky, the other occupant of that room, has been called many things, both during her lifetime and after it. For some she was an "explosive madcap." For others, like the psychical researcher Richard Hodgson, she was "one of the most accomplished, ingenious, and interesting impostors in history." For the founder of Anthroposophy, Rudolf Steiner, she was a "cheeky creature," an "electrically-charged Leyden jar" who exhibited a "lack of consistency in external behaviour." For the poet W. B. Yeats, who knew her in her last days in London, she was like an Irish peasant woman. For her early biographer John Symonds, she was "one of the most remarkable women who ever lived," yet her later biographer, Peter Washington, called her a "badly wrapped parcel." And for the novelist Kurt Vonnegut, writing in *McCall's* magazine in 1970, she was "the Founding Mother of the Occult in America."

As with many complex, vital, and fascinating characters, all of these assessments are in some ways true, yet all fail to grasp the full essence of this enormous personality. HPB, as she became known to her followers, was as capacious an individual as possible. If, as the writer Henry Miller once said, we should "live life to the hilt," she had certainly done that, and more. But on that September day she embraced a destiny that would transcend even her own fantastic life and, quite frankly, affect the world. Because it was then that she, Olcott, and Judge decided to found the Theosophical Society, arguably the most important spiritual and esoteric organization the West has ever known. It is no exaggeration to say that if it weren't for these three people, much of what we know as modern spirituality, consciousness exploration, and alternative thought —not to mention our inexhaustible fascination with the wisdom of the East—might not have arrived, or at least might have taken much longer to than it did. By the time of Blavatsky's death in 1891, the Theosophical movement had spread from New York to India, Europe, and beyond. And by the early years of the twentieth century, it was a force, as the saying goes, to be reckoned with, informing major developments in politics, art, religion, and much more. The poet T. S. Eliot, the artist Wassily Kandinsky, the inventor Thomas Edison, the creator of Oz, L. Frank Baum, and Mohandas Gandhi were only some of the people who over the years sat—figuratively or otherwise—at the incomparable Madame's feet.

Helena Petrovna Blavatsky was born Helena von Hahn in 1831 in Ekaterinoslav, in what was then Russia and is now the Ukraine. Her mother, Helena Fadeyeva, was a popular novelist, writing under the pen name Zeneida Riva. Her father, Peter von Hahn, was a colonel and descended from a family of German nobility. Helena's sister, Vera Zhelikhovksy, wrote children's stories, as well as weird occult fiction, something HPB's detractors say she did herself when pointing to her vast works of mystical philosophy, *Isis Unveiled* and *The Secret Doctrine*. (She did, in fact, write some occult short stories.) When her mother died at the age of twenty-eight, Helena was only eleven, and she was raised by her grandmother in a cultured and spiritual milieu. This didn't prevent her from becoming something of a tomboy, an irrepressible, mischievous spirit more at home in the forests and fields than with dolls, who nevertheless devoured the vast occult library of her great-grandfather, the Freemason Prince Pavel Dolgorukov. Although it wasn't until she had passed forty and had traveled around the world that HPB revealed the source of her wisdom, she claimed that from an early age she had had meetings with her "master," Morya, a strange figure who appeared in her childhood dreams and whom she would later meet in the flesh in London's Hyde Park and then again in Tibet. The master was one of a group of highly evolved beings who guided mankind in its development and whose emissary it was Helena's destiny to become. But that was sometime ahead, and before then she would take more than one rollicking roller-coaster ride.

When Helena was seventeen, she married a man more than twice her age, the vice-governor of Yerevan in Armenia, Nikifor Vladimirovich Blavatsky. One motivation seems to have been the belief that no one else would have her, although, until she gained weight in her later years, she was attractive, something that comes through in her portraits, and, in any case, her appearance was always striking. The marriage was never consummated, and although they were never divorced, Helena soon left Nikifor for the great unknown. It is thought Blavatsky remained celibate throughout her life—sex, she said, was "beastly"—and to counter later accusations of promiscuity (she was also rumored to be lesbian and a transvestite), she produced a doctor's certificate establishing that a fall from a horse during her time as a circus bareback rider had made it impossible for her to have intercourse. The place, she said, was "filled up with some crooked cucumber," and she was frank enough to prove it. That flight from her crestfallen husband was the start of her decade-long *Wanderjahre*, a journey into adventure that her contemporary Jules Verne would restrict to fiction. For young Helena, it was everyday life.

Between 1848, when she abandoned Nikifor, and 1858, when she briefly returned to Russia, HPB's boot heels, as Bob Dylan sang, went wandering. Egypt, France, Canada, England, South America, Germany, Mexico, India, Greece, and Tibet were some of the main stops on her journey. Her passport, if she had one, must have taken a beating. Many of a mystical bent in the West have gone on prodigious voyages. In the sixteenth century, the travels of Paracelsus, the father of Western alternative medicine, were legendary, and in more recent times figures like the enigmatic Greco-Armenian spiritual teacher G. I. Gurdjieff and the dark magician Aleister Crowley trekked into more than one unusual place. But Blavatsky was a woman, just out of her teens, and for a woman to travel alone at all in those days was unusual; for one to enter Tibet was unheard of. Even after the British expedition in 1903 led by Francis Younghusband, in which more than a thousand Tibetans were slaughtered, for many years Tibet was off-limits to most Westerners. HPB herself said she was turned away a few times before finally crossing the threshold, an accomplishment echoed more than half a century later in 1924 by another intrepid woman, the Belgian-French writer, explorer, and Buddhist Alexandra David-Néel.

Blavatsky's tenure in Tibet has always been contested; the controversy won't stop here, but some of her other adventures suggest it was more than possible. In 1867 she was wounded while fighting with the Italian liberator Giuseppe Garibaldi against the papal army and the French at the battle of Mentana, a sacrifice that led to a friendship with Giuseppe Mazzini, leader of the revolutionary movement Young Italy. And if that wasn't enough to qualify as "living dangerously," in 1871 she was one of the few survivors of the wreck of the *Eumonia*, a sea disaster as famous in its day as the *Titanic*. She washed ashore in Cairo, and it's believed she started her career as a spirit medium then, although she had exhibited psychic powers from the start. At any rate, it was then that she started holding séances.

From Cairo she went to France, and it was in Paris that the masters pointed her in the right direction. Go west, they said, so she sailed for New York. When she arrived in the summer of 1873 at the age of forty-two, she was penniless—she had crossed the Atlantic in steerage—and for a time lived in hostels and cheap boardinghouses, scratching out a living by sewing purses. But it wasn't long before she showed her resourcefulness. Reading Colonel Olcott's series of articles in the *Daily Graphic* about a haunting at a farm in Chittenden, Vermont—he had developed an interest in spiritualism while learning to farm in Ohio—Blavatsky determined to meet him. Her decision to ensnare Olcott in many ways resembles Gurdjieff's later decision to "entrap" his disciple Ouspensky, who was also a journalist; both "crazy gurus" seemed to need a respectable PR man devoted to the cause. When the robust Helena approached the cautious Olcott at the farm, it was a case of platonic love at first sight. The retiring, conventional colonel was smitten, as much by Helena's fiery Garibaldi shirt (a bright red blouse with military embroidery, a souvenir of the barricades) as by her chutzpah. (As one writer remarked, she was "capable of colourful and imaginative profanity," another characteristic she shared with Gurdjieff.) She proceeded to dominate the séances, introducing her own crew of spirits—appropriately Russian—and made it clear that a real contender had arrived.

Spiritualism had been a part of American culture since 1848, when the Fox sisters of Hydesville, New York, discovered they could communicate with the spirit of a dead man. By the time HPB appeared, it had even entered politics. In 1872, Victoria Woodhull, another extraordinary nineteenth-century woman, had run for president on a spiritualist–free love–feminist–socialist ticket; needless to say, she didn't win. But spiritualism was running out of steam, and when Blavatsky and Olcott formed their occult alliance after Olcott received a message from one of HPB's masters advising him to leave his unsatisfactory marriage and live with Helena, it was clear something new was wanted. Blavatsky herself had grown bored with table rapping and levitating tambourines. She could easily produce phenomena at will, and, unlike most psychics, was not a mere "medium" but had control of her "powers." Nevertheless, her masters had counseled that she was being primed for something greater. She and the colonel agreed, and their first attempt was to found what they called the Miracle Club. When this didn't produce the required miracle, they looked for something else.

Part of that something else was Blavatsky's massive tome, *Isis Unveiled*, a fourteen-hundred-page epic of occult wisdom, which she started writing in 1875, with references nabbed from the astral plane. When it was published two years later, in 1877, it sold out its first printing overnight. Although some papers panned the work— one reviewer called it "a dish of hash"—*The New York Herald* said it was "one of the most remarkable productions of the century," and *The Boston Evening Transcript* argued that its author had "read more, seen more, and thought more than most wise men." Its eager readers agreed. People today familiar with Theosophy's better-known Eastern character may be surprised at the more Western, Egyptian esotericism that fills *Isis Unveiled*'s many pages. For a time in her career, Egypt, and not the Himalayas, was the focus of Blavatsky's mystic yearnings, a popular spot, as the contemporaneous Hermetic Brotherhood of Luxor, led by the mysterious Max Théon, showed. Blavatsky herself spoke of a mysterious "brotherhood of Luxor," and Colonel Olcott received his mystic messages from a certain Tuitit Bey. These messages themselves were the first of a series of "precipitated" (i.e., materialized) letters for which HPB would soon become famous. Later epistles would fall from thin air and apprise HPB's colleagues and skeptics of her masters' wishes.

It is impossible to summarize *Isis Unveiled* here, except to say it was one of the first works of occultism to argue that magic was not some mindless superstition palmed off on the gullible, but a profound wisdom and science known to the ancients, yet lost to modern materialism. It's an idea still popular today, as a look at the works of Graham Hancock and other authors that make much the same argument shows. For much of her theme, Blavatsky drew on the writings of Éliphas Lévi and Edward Bulwer-Lytton, whose novel *Zanoni* weaves Rosicrucian and Hermetic motifs into a historical romance. She also quoted—or plagiarized, depending on your perspective—dozens of other authorities, from Plato and *The Egyptian Book of the Dead* to Schopenhauer and Giordano Bruno. Whatever we may think of *Isis Unveiled*, its historical importance is undeniable, as it contained the first detailed critique of Darwin's recently enshrined version of evolution. Samuel Butler— of *Erewhon* fame—published *Life and Habit*, the first of his several vigorous attacks on Darwinian theory, in 1878, but Blavatsky beat him to it. Her central argument is that the transition from monkey to man is only part of the more significant evolution of men and women into gods, a transformation that embraces the entire cosmos. As one writer remarked, instead of opposing religion to scientific fact, Blavatsky "subsumes those facts into a grand synthesis that makes religious wisdom not the enemy of scientific knowledge but its final goal."

At the same time as Blavatsky scoured the astral plane for quotable material, a suggestion at a lecture given at her apartment—nicknamed "the Lamasery" because of its exotic decor—triggered the second phase of that elusive "something else." After hearing a talk about the "secret canon of proportions" the ancient Egyptians used to construct the pyramids (like spiritualism, pyramidology was another late nineteenth-century craze), Colonel Olcott had the brainstorm of forming a society that would study such things. HPB and the others present agreed, and a week later she, Olcott, and Judge met again and the Theosophical Society was born. The name was not new. *Theosophy*, meaning the "wisdom of the gods," had been used by Neoplatonic philosophers in the Alexandria of the third century AD, and also by the gnomic seventeenth-century Hermetic cobbler, Jacob Boehme. With HPB and the colonel, however, it would take on a somewhat different sense. The society's mission statement set out its goals: to promote the universal brotherhood of humanity, regardless of race, creed, color, or sex; to study ancient and modern religions, philosophies, and sciences; and to investigate the unexplained phenomena of nature and the hidden powers in man. With its multifaith, multicultural emphasis, the Theosophical Society anticipated our own pluralistic sensibility by more than a century. And, as mentioned, its belief in a lost, ancient wisdom is still going strong.

Although the new society gathered some initial interest, later bolstered by the success of *Isis Unveiled* and Olcott's involvement in one of the earliest cremations in America, by the end of 1878, the "chums," as Olcott and Blavatsky called themselves, were running out of resources and seriously needed some new direction. Perhaps the masters had tired of Luxor, or perhaps Egypt was by this time old hat. Whatever it was, the needle on the Madame's mystic compass began to bypass the Sphinx and turn toward points east, and the chums shifted their gaze toward India. Blavatsky had already introduced Eastern themes in the second part of *Isis Unveiled*, but a perhaps more encouraging motive was the invitation from Swami Dayananda Sarasvati, leader of a Hindu movement called Arya Samaj, to come to India and unite their new society with his; an acquaintance of Olcott's had told the swami about Theosophy, and he felt it was in tune with his teachings. Daniel Dunglas Home, the most successful medium of the age, had only recently made some damaging remarks about the Madame, who, according to some reports, had been his assistant for a time, so perhaps a journey to the

East was in order. After selling most of their possessions to placate creditors, and following the orders of the masters, who would soon be called Mahatmas, on December 17, 1878, the chums boarded ship for Bombay (today's Mumbai). Blavatsky's US citizenship had come through just a few months earlier, but she would never see America again. Abner Doubleday, Civil War hero and purported inventor of baseball, was left in charge of the New York branch, while Judge later became head of the society in America.

When the chums reached India in February 1879, the subcontinent was still in thrall to the British Raj, and the natives knew less about Hinduism and its great works, like the Upanishads and Bhagavad Gita, than most New Age folk do today. Two cultured and famous Westerners who embraced the immortal wisdom of the East and rejected Christianity (which was busily being foisted on the Hindus) were welcome, and soon HPB knew they had made the right choice. Swami Dayananda, however, grew to regret it, as Theosophy soon eclipsed the Arya Samaj, and the two went their separate ways. Blavatsky and Olcott's magazine, *The Theosophist*, sold incredibly well, and many flocked to join the society. Even HPB's powers seemed to have increased. Among other feats, she caused a shower of roses, made a lamp flame grow larger and smaller at will, materialized cups and saucers, and located a brooch lost years before by her hostess. These miracles garnered much publicity, but Blavatsky herself thought them unimportant. She made a hefty social and political impact when she brought A. P. Sinnett, editor of the influential *Allahabad Pioneer*, into the fold. Sinnett's books, *The Occult World* and *Esoteric Buddhism*, spread the teachings to a huge readership, including a shy young Austrian scholar named Rudolf Steiner and an Irish poet named Yeats. Another catch was A. O. Home, a high-ranking civil servant who later organized the first Indian National Congress. Blavatsky's Hinduphilia and contempt for the British, who thought she was a Russian spy, set the snowball rolling; and some years later, when her successor, the Fabian suffragette Annie Besant, arrived on India's shores, Theosophy was at the heart of the independence movement.

Both Gandhi and Jawaharlal Nehru became Theosophists and later praised the society for the immense good it did their nation.

For the first five years, India was an unqualified success for Theosophy. Olcott was so successful in bringing Buddhism to Buddhists that in 1968, Sri Lanka—in Olcott's day, Ceylon—issued a commemorative stamp in his honor, and the growing Theosophical ranks were a serious rival to imported Christianity.

Yet it was Blavatsky's own good nature that proved her undoing. Emma Coulombe, a woman she had befriended in Cairo, wrote to her from Ceylon, telling of hard times. Blavatsky invited her and her husband to keep house for her in Bombay. This proved disastrous. In 1884, Blavatsky left India to visit France and England. In London the Society for Psychical Research (SPR) suggested they investigate her claims. Sensational reports of the "precipitated letters" from her master—not Morya this time, but Koot Hoomi—had been in newspapers around the world, and they were eager to verify their authenticity. But back in India Emma Coulombe, peeved by some assumed slight, told the editor of a Christian missionary magazine that the whole thing was faked. The Mahatma letters were "precipitated" by being slipped through cracks in the ceiling, and the figure of Koot Hoomi—often seen by astounded visitors—was really Blavatsky, wearing a model of the Mahatma on her shoulders. There was other chicanery as well, and remembering her scathing remarks about Christian missionaries, the *Christian College Magazine* was only too happy to blow the whistle on the Madame.

The scandal reached the SPR, and to this day it's unclear if the evidence for fraud their investigator Richard Hodgson allegedly found was planted or authentic. Either way, he issued a damning report, and HPB's reputation suffered badly, although the SPR itself retracted his report a century later, saying it was prejudiced and unreliable. Although she was not above hoodwinking when necessary, it's difficult to study Blavatsky's life and not conclude she was genuine. She returned to India to defend her reputation, but to avoid being drawn into a legal battle that would inevitably turn into a show trial, she soon left again, never to return.

On the road again, Blavatsky found herself in Italy, Germany, and Switzerland. She finally roosted in England. She was by this time ill, suffering from kidney failure brought on by her weight and other stress. Contrary to much current spiritual thought, HPB didn't give a hoot for her health; her cholesterol levels were scandalous and she chain-smoked incessantly. She may have known her days were numbered and so decided to write another monstrous tome, *The Secret Doctrine*, Theosophy's bible. Even longer than *Isis Unveiled*, *The Secret Doctrine* expounded a monumental synthesis of science, religion, and philosophy that remains thrilling and controversial enough to fuel many a metaphysical discussion, although, as one writer remarked, it is in many ways "a muddy torrent carrying all kinds of strange objects on its surface." Blavatsky threw together a smorgasbord of occult and mystical teachings about humanity and the cosmos in a way that again precludes summary, speaking of the mysterious *Book of Dzyan*, written in the lost language of Senzar, and its profound revelations about human and cosmic evolution. The universe has been created and destroyed several times—an idea that science came to only much later—and we modern humans are only one of a series of races to inhabit the planet, our history going back to ancient Atlantis, Lemuria, and beyond. Reincarnation was a fundamental theme, and with it the eventual evolution of humanity into the divine.

When the book appeared in 1888, it fed the ravenous hunger many Westerners felt for some spiritual and religious meaning in a world increasingly seen to be little more than an accident. Darwin had shown us to be merely "trousered apes"; and, in any case, the universe itself was rolling toward its "heat death," an inescapable outcome of entropy, in which the innumerable galaxies would flatten out into a formless cosmic puddle like a lukewarm cup of coffee. Having given so much ground to science that it had nothing to offer against these "facts," the church had become little more than an empty shell. Blavatsky's strange, exotic blend of hidden Mahatmas, supernatural powers, cosmic evolution, past lives, sunken continents, and prehistoric civilizations struck more than a chord in the fin de siècle mind; it offered a powerful counter-narrative to the doom and gloom that mainstream science served on tap. Many who rejected the church but refused science's cosmic inconsequence gravitated toward HPB and the Theosophical view. To this day both she and the Theosophical Society are yet to receive the credit they are due for providing a vital alternative to the sense of purposelessness that characterized the last years of the nineteenth century.

Blavatsky's last days were spent in St. John's Wood, London, where she was wheeled around in a kind of perambulator. She died on May 8, 1891, a day celebrated in Theosophical communities as White Lotus Day. She was sixty and had taken the world by storm, and her last words are characteristically blunt: "Don't let my last incarnation be a failure." Chances are we will not see her like again, but with her help, anyone today can remove the veil from Isis and discover where the secret wisdom can be found.

CHAPTER SEVEN

Rudolf Steiner:
The Dweller on the Threshold

The most enigmatic figure to emerge from the occult revival of the
early twentieth century was also the most successful: the Austrian
"spiritual scientist" Rudolf Steiner (1861–1925). Although many of his
contemporaries were outwardly more eccentric—think of Madame
Blavatsky, Gurdjieff, or Aleister Crowley—it's precisely Steiner's sobriety
that is so striking, making him seem somewhat out of place in the often
flamboyant world of the esoteric.

We generally associate ideas of the occult, higher consciousness, and
spiritual worlds with exotic, extraordinary characters with something
of the trickster about them; Blavatsky, Gurdjieff, and Crowley would
certainly fall into this category. Steiner was precisely the opposite.
Standing at the lectern with his pince-nez in hand, he projected an
image of irreproachable rectitude. Steiner was earnestness incarnate,
his one gesture of bohemian extravagance the flowing bow ties he was
fond of wearing, a remnant of his early student days. Where Blavatsky,
Gurdjieff, and Crowley each took pains to present a formidable self-
image, there was something simple and peasantlike about Steiner.
Combined with this wholesomeness was an encyclopedic erudition. If
we were to use an archetype to describe Steiner, it would have to be that
of "the Professor"—or more precisely, "the Doctor," as he was known
by those around him. Commenting on her magnum opus, *The Secret
Doctrine*, Madame Blavatsky once remarked that she "wrote, wrote,
wrote" as the Wandering Jew "walks, walks, walks." Steiner too wrote a

great deal, but his main mode of disseminating his ideas was lecturing, and in the years between 1900 and 1925 he lectured, lectured, lectured, delivering more than six thousand talks across Europe.

In a dry and often pedantic style, Steiner informed his audience of the results of his spiritual research, his "supersensible" readings of the occult history of the world made available to him through what is called the Akashic Record. In matter-of-fact terms, he introduced them to his teaching, Anthroposophy, telling them along the way about ancient Atlantis, life after death, astral and etheric bodies, the true meaning of Christianity, and much, much more. Yet this humble, self-effacing character became one of the most influential, and simultaneously vilified, forces in the spiritual and cultural life of early twentieth-century Europe, and his ideas are still relevant today. Steiner's efforts to lead "the Spiritual in the human being to the Spiritual in the Universe" have produced remarkably concrete results. Since his death, more than a thousand schools around the world work with Steiner's pedagogical principles, not to mention the many special-needs schools working along lines developed by Steiner a century ago. There are also the hundreds of biodynamic farms employing Steiner's agricultural insights, developed decades in advance of our interest in ecology and organic foods. The practical application of Steiner's ideas had also informed very successful avenues in holistic healing, the arts, architecture, economics, religion, and other areas.

Given these achievements in the "real world," which certainly exceed those of other esoteric teachers, why isn't Steiner better known? You would reasonably expect the average educated person to have some idea of who, say, Jung is, or Krishnamurti, or the Dalai Lama; possibly even Blavatsky, Gurdjieff, or Crowley. But Steiner? He remains something of a mystery, a name associated with a handful of different disciplines and endeavors but not solidly linked to any one thing. He remains, as one of his most eloquent apologists, the British writer and thinker Owen Barfield, called him, "the best kept secret of the twentieth century." It's certainly time that he was better known.

Rudolf Steiner was born on February 27, 1861, in the small rural town of Kraljevec in what was then Hungary but is today part of Croatia. His father was a telegraph operator for the Southern Austrian Railway, and Steiner spent his first years amidst magnificent scenery: mountain ranges and green plains were his playgrounds. Steiner felt that it was significant that he grew up in a part of Europe where East meets West, as it was also significant that childhood had an equal measure of natural beauty and modern technology—at the time, both the railways and the telegraph were relatively new innovations. In *Knowledge of the Higher Worlds and Its Attainment* (1905), Steiner relates that a crucial experience on the path of higher consciousness is an encounter with the Guardian of the Threshold, a spiritual being embodying one's unredeemed karma. Well before his career as an esoteric teacher, Steiner was himself a dweller on several thresholds, having one foot in the mysteries of nature, the other in the methodology of science. It was this combination of mystic visionary and disciplined thinker that gave Steiner's later career its peculiar character.

When Steiner was eight, his father was transferred to Neudörfl, near the border with lower Austria. An argument with the local teacher led his father to educate the boy himself, and this meant that he spent a great deal of time on his own at the railway station where his father worked. Young Steiner was deeply introverted; as he admits in his *Autobiography* (1925), he had great difficulty relating to the outer world. He also had an inquisitive mind and was obsessed with many questions the adults he knew seemed unable to answer. This subjectivity might have taken a morbid turn were it not for his discovery of mathematics. When Steiner came upon a book of geometry, it was a revelation. "That one can work out forms which are seen purely inwardly, independent of the outer senses, gave me a feeling of deep contentment. I found consolation for the loneliness caused by the many unanswered questions. To be able to grasp something purely spiritual brought me an inner joy. I know that through geometry I first experienced happiness."

Steiner's joy upon discovering geometry may strike us as odd, yet the experience was essential in getting him through an early crisis. What impressed Steiner so greatly about geometry was that it seemed to offer proof that within the mind there existed a kind of "soul space," an inner equivalent of the external space of the natural world. The soul space was "the setting for spiritual beings and events." Thoughts for the young Steiner were not "mere pictures we form of things"; they were rather the "revelations of a spiritual world seen on the stage of the soul." Geometry, Steiner believed, although produced by the human mind, had an objective reality independent of it, and for him this meant that the soul space in which it was revealed was also real. Rather precocious stuff, perhaps, but Steiner's early years included an event that made him question the outer world's monopoly on reality.

One day at the railway station, he had a paranormal experience, an early manifestation of his psychic abilities. Sitting in the waiting room, he saw a strange woman enter; although he didn't know her, he felt she resembled other members of his family. Standing in the middle of the room, the woman spoke to the boy. "Try to help me as much as you can—now as well as in later life," she said. Then she walked into the stove and disappeared. Steiner decided not to tell his parents, afraid that they would scold him for lying. But he noticed that his father was sad, and he later discovered that a female relative who lived in the neighboring town had committed suicide at the same time that he had had his vision. Although he doesn't mention this episode in his *Autobiography*, in a lecture given in Berlin in 1913 Steiner spoke of the experience. Speaking in the third person, he told his audience: "From that time onward a soul-life began to develop in the boy, which made him entirely conscious of worlds from which not only external trees or mountain speak to the human soul, but also the Beings who live behind them." This early experience marked for Steiner the beginning of a lifelong involvement with the dead. Much of his later esoteric teaching involves accounts of the soul's experiences in the afterlife and of the machinery of karma and reincarnation, the balancing of the spiritual books that casts the departed back into the stream of life in order to complete their tasks. While other boys of his age were fantasizing about the Austrian equivalent of cowboys and Indians, Steiner was preoccupied with the reality of the spirit worlds and the soul's encounter with the beings that inhabit them.

Later, as a young man, Steiner would on two occasions have unusual opportunities to verify some of his ideas about the meaning of death. Twice he would come into intimate contact with families in which the father was a recluse who would die soon after Steiner made their acquaintance. Yet on both occasions, although never actually meeting the man, Steiner formed a profound intuitive relation with the deceased, so deep and insightful in fact that he was asked by both families to give the funeral orations. Later still, during his years as an esoteric teacher, Steiner informed his followers that one means of helping the dead in their spiritual journeys was to read to them from his writings.

When Steiner was eighteen, his father was transferred once again, this time to Inzersdorf. His new location had the advantage of being close to Vienna, and it was decided that Steiner would study at the technical school there. Although he had leanings toward literature and philosophy, he chose instead to work toward becoming a science teacher. One day on the train to Vienna, he met a man who would have a profound influence on his life. Felix Koguzki was an herb gatherer who traveled to Vienna regularly to sell his wares. It's not known how they fell into conversation, but the teenaged Steiner soon discovered that this simple, uneducated man had strange experiences like his own, and a deep, personal knowledge of the other worlds. Koguzki was the first person with whom he could speak about his spiritual visions, and their talks boosted Steiner's confidence; more than likely, they also convinced him that he wasn't crazy.

Around the same time, Steiner had an encounter with another individual whose name has not come down to us. Steiner refers to him only as "the Master." The French writer Edouard Schuré, author of the bestselling *Great Initiates* (1889) and later a friend and follower of Steiner, remarked that the Master was "one of those potent personalities who are on Earth to fulfil a mission under the mask of some homely occupation." Steiner had by this time read widely in philosophy, specifically the German Idealists, and had worked his way through Hegel, Schelling, and several others, absorbing Kant's *Critique of Pure Reason* during his history class, which bored him. Steiner was obsessed, then and later, with refuting scientific materialism, and this became the impulse that drove his philosophical studies. What little we know of the Master is that he pointed out some passages in the work of Johann Gottlieb Fichte, one of Kant's most important followers, which helped Steiner in his quest. Fichte's work focused on the centrality of the human ego, the "I," the locus of consciousness and the self that scientific materialism argued was mere illusion. Steiner's spiritual experiences convinced him that this was palpably false and the "I," rather than being an illusion, was a concrete, irreducible reality. For the next twenty years, until Steiner's reinvention as a spiritual leader, his work would focus on developing a methodical epistemology proving this fact.

The single most important influence on his ideas, however, was the work of Johann Wolfgang von Goethe. Goethe is best known for his drama *Faust* (1808–1832), which takes a cautionary tale about a pact with the Devil and transforms it into an archetype of Western consciousness. Although he's never enjoyed the same reputation among English speakers, Goethe is one of the Olympians of Western literature, sharing the top shelf with Plato, Dante, and Shakespeare (Jung too thought Goethe a key figure, even to the extent of sometimes believing that he, Jung, was an illegitimate descendent of the great man.) Often regarded as the last true Renaissance man, Goethe was not just a giant of literature but also a statesman, traveler, and, most important for Steiner, a scientist, making important contributions to botany, anatomy, mineralogy, and optics. Through his literature tutor Karl Schröer, who opened his mind to Goethe's importance, Steiner was offered what must have seemed the chance of a lifetime. At twenty-two, he was headhunted as the editor of Goethe's scientific writings for a major edition of the polymath's work.

For an unknown rural scholar to be offered such a position might seem unusual, but the general consensus on Goethe's scientific musings at this point was that they were useless as science and dreary as literature; in truth, no one else wanted the job of editing them. Aside from his early success in proving that the human upper jaw contained the intermaxillary bone found in other mammals—Goethe was, in a different way, an evolutionist long before Darwin—most scientists found Goethe's attempts to disprove Newton's theory of color, or to demonstrate the existence of what he called the *Urpflanze*, the archetypal plant from which others emerged, muddleheaded if not insane. Yet for Steiner, Goethe science was the prototype for what would become his own phenomenology of the spirit worlds. Instead of the conventional scientist's cold, dispassionate eye regarding the world as mere matter, passive to his intrusions, Goethe called instead for "objective imagination," an active participation in the reality under scrutiny. The subjectivity of the scientist—his state of consciousness—was vastly more important than the increasingly hair-splitting exactitude provided by his instruments. This "objective imagination" became for Steiner the basis for his own "supersensible cognition."

Steiner's work on Goethe opened many doors. One led to Weimar, Goethe's city, where he was asked to work on the Goethe Archive, another prestigious task. Although Steiner found few congenial colleagues, the work had other compensations. He was introduced to the city's literary and cultural life and made many acquaintances. One in particular led to a momentous meeting. Elizabeth Forster Nietzsche, sister of the ill-fated philosopher, approached Steiner to work with her in establishing a Nietzsche archive. This led to Elizabeth introducing Steiner to her brother, who had been insane from syphilis for several years. Elizabeth had taken to dressing the defenseless Friedrich in a toga and positioning him by the window, where his blank stare and unkempt appearance provided the impression of a great prophet. Steiner, aware of

Nietzsche's madness, was nevertheless impressed—not with the figure before him, but with its spiritual aura. He saw Nietzsche's soul "hovering over his head, infinitely beautiful in its spiritual sight." It was a soul that "brought from former lives on Earth golden riches of great spirituality."

If mention of Nietzsche's soul brimming with "golden riches of great spirituality" suggests to readers familiar with the author of *Beyond Good and Evil* and *The Antichrist* that Steiner was as ignorant of Nietzsche's philosophy as his sister Elizabeth notoriously was, they should have a look at Steiner's book *Friedrich Nietzsche: Fighter for Freedom* (1895), a remarkably perceptive study that at times even reads like Nietzsche. Throughout his career, Steiner had an uncanny knack for entering into and defending the ideas of thinkers with whom he had profound disagreements, like the staunch materialist Ernst Haeckel—a critical sympathy that often led to much misunderstanding.

When his work at Weimar was ending, rather than embark on an academic career (Steiner had received his doctorate in philosophy during his stay and could easily have found a comfortable niche somewhere), he decided instead to move to Berlin, home of Germany's nascent avant-garde. He had by this time published what many believe to be his most important book, *The Philosophy of Freedom* (1894), an exhilarating if often difficult work of epistemology that Steiner believed established beyond doubt the reality of the human "I." Others, like the influential philosopher Karl Robert Eduard von Hartmann, author of the once immensely popular *Philosophy of the Unconscious*, were less convinced and suggested he had muddled the question. Steiner, however, was undaunted and believed he had a mission to disseminate his ideas. He also needed to find work. Although his followers tend to see Steiner's life as the undeviating unfolding of a preordained destiny—and Steiner himself, we must admit, contributes to this belief—like the rest of us, he was looking for his place in the world and the means to get on in it. He was also filled (rightly) with the conviction of his own genius. The literary and cultural world of Berlin might offer opportunities not available elsewhere.

Steiner, however, made the thoroughly impractical decision of buying a moribund periodical, *The Magazine for Literature*. His previous brief catastrophic experience in Vienna as an editor of a political magazine seemingly forgotten, Steiner proceeded to run the already failing *Magazine for Literature* into the ground, alienating its readers with his persistent exhortations regarding the spiritual life. In the age of Strindberg, Wilde, Ibsen, Wedekind, and Shaw, Steiner's Idealism seemed a stale leftover from a forgotten time.

Yet, although he bemoaned the burden destiny had placed on him, Steiner seems to have enjoyed hobnobbing with bohemians: his acquaintances included poets, playwrights, novelists, and political activists. In fact, his reputation among the demimonde caused academics to cancel their subscriptions, and Steiner earned the unique distinction of being the one esoteric teacher (as far as I know) to have a periodical banned in tsarist Russia because its editor was known to socialize with anarchists. It was also in Berlin that Steiner married his first wife, although one gets the impression that his relationship with Anna Eunicke was little more than platonic. Anna had been Steiner's landlady in Weimar, and when he moved to Berlin she followed him. There he moved in with her again and, almost as an afterthought, married her in 1899 in a civil ceremony. (It was in the Eunicke household in Weimar that Steiner had had one of his experiences with the death of a reclusive father.) Anna, not particularly well-educated or cultured, was apparently very happy to have Herr Doctor Steiner under her roof; Steiner, for his part, thus avoided the "misery of living alone," as well as that of the cheap lodgings and bad food he had endured up till then. Anna was ten years older than Rudolf, and their relationship raises the question of Steiner's sexuality, of which there is no mention in the entire 406 pages of his *Autobiography*. I do have it on the authority of one Steiner scholar, Christopher Bamford, that the Doctor was indeed celibate.

But it was in Berlin that Steiner's real career began. For a time he seemed willing to speak to any group who would listen to him. He lectured on history and other subjects at the Workingman's College, surreptitiously slipping large doses of Idealism to budding Marxist materialists. He also lectured to the Giordano Bruno Society and The Coming Day, a quasi-Nietzschean cultural group. He managed, however, to alienate all of these organizations (as well as Anna Eunicke, whom he soon left) when he accepted a request to lecture to the Berlin Theosophical Society. For years, Steiner had tried to express his insights into the spiritual worlds under the cover of philosophy. Now, at the turn of the century and the age of forty, he decided to forgo the camouflage and speak directly of his experiences.

Steiner quickly rose to prominence among the Theosophists and was soon made head of the society's branch. One member of his audience was particularly struck. Marie von Sivers, who became Steiner's second wife in 1914, was a Baltic Russian actress. She asked if it weren't time for a new spiritual movement to arise in Europe. More to the point, didn't Steiner think he should lead it? Steiner did, but he insisted that any such movement would be firmly based on Western esoteric sources. Steiner had recently passed through a spiritual crisis, which convinced him that the "Christ event" was the single most important incident in human history. He had no time for Eastern wisdom or mystic Mahatmas. He then more or less adopted the cosmic evolutionary framework of Madame Blavatsky's *Secret Doctrine* and informed it with large helpings of German Idealist philosophy and Christian mysticism, developing a peculiarly idiosyncratic neo-Rosicrucian system of esoteric thought, aided by his own readings of the Akashic Record. In light of this, it's difficult to ignore the occult historian James Webb's remark that Steiner joined the Theosophical Society in order to take it over.

His relationship to the society was rocky, and in 1913 he and its head, the ex-Fabian Annie Besant, came to rhetorical blows over C. W. Leadbeater's advocacy of the Indian boy Jiddu Krishnamurti as the second coming of Christ. Steiner was disgusted at the idea, and even more so at Leadbeater's known pedophilic predilections. He demanded Besant's resignation; she retaliated by excommunicating him. Steiner left with much of his flock—by this time several thousand—and started his own group, the Anthroposophical Society. As opposed to Theosophy, which spoke of the wisdom of the gods, Anthroposophy was concerned with the wisdom of the human being.

Practically the first thing Steiner did was to build a temple for his new movement. Land was secured in Dornach, Switzerland, and during World War I Steiner gathered a community of followers from several different countries to construct the Goetheanum, a weirdly beautiful fusion of art nouveau and expressionist architecture that Steiner himself designed. His lecturing was curtailed by the fighting, but his greatest popularity came with the war's end. Steiner's plan to reconstruct Europe, *The Threefold Commonwealth* (1922), sold some eighty thousand copies in its first edition, and audiences for his public appearances were now in the thousands; on one occasion the crowds outside a Berlin auditorium were so great they stopped traffic. This period, however, also saw the start of the anti-Steiner campaign that would plague him henceforth. Practically everybody hated him: Catholics, Protestants, Marxists, and proto-Nazis, not to mention other esotericists. There were at least two attempts on his life, and the number of occult attacks fomented by the "black brotherhoods" is unknown. One clear victory from this time was the establishment of the first Steiner school in Stuttgart in 1919—the first of what became known as Waldorf schools. Based on pedagogical principles developed over decades of tutoring—in Vienna he had cured a retarded hydrocephalic boy to the extent that the child grew up to earn a medical degree—Steiner's educational ideas earned him deserved renown and an international reputation among experts that continues today.

Steiner endured vilification in the press and disruption at his lectures with equanimity, but one victim of the attacks was, many believe, the Goetheanum, which burned to the ground on New Year's Eve 1922. Arson by right-wing proto-Nazis is the common assumption, although an electrical fault remains a possibility. In any case, a decade's effort, not to mention an architectural wonder, was lost overnight: the building was made of the same wood as that used in making violins and burned fiercely. Steiner took the tragedy as a sign that some changes in the Anthroposophical Society were necessary. His original occult teachings, based on the idea of an evolution of consciousness and the ability to achieve "supersensible thinking," were, he felt, obscured by the success of subsequent initiatives. Steiner education, the Christian Community (a religious group using Steiner's ideas), the Threefold Movement for social change, eurythmy—a form of what he called "visible speech"—and newer developments like biodynamic farming and Anthroposophical medicine were taking center stage. Steiner had attracted many younger followers after the war eager to rebuild society, and these clashed with his older, more esoterically inclined devotees. Bickering within the Anthroposophical Society, whose numbers had swollen in the postwar years, threatened to undo much that had been achieved. On the first anniversary of the Goetheanum's destruction, Steiner announced plans for a second temple; it stands today in Dornach, defiantly made of concrete. He also told his followers that he was reconstructing the society as well. Although he had not previously even been a member of the society, remaining only its spiritual guide and adviser, he now declared himself president of the newly formed General Anthroposophical Society, which, although most successful in Germany, today has branches around the world.

Steiner's last years were spent in sowing as many seeds as possible for future work; they were also darkened by his belief in a coming world conflagration, when the archangel Michael, overseer of the current stage of human consciousness, would face off against the power of Ahriman, a spiritual being who seeks to prevent humanity's development. Steiner spoke ominously of the incarnation of Ahriman, an Antichrist-like figure whose display of miraculous powers would precede a catastrophic "war of all against all." Steiner believed this unavoidable destiny would take some time to unfold—Ahriman is scheduled to arrive in the 3000s—but many of his followers suspect that in recent years the process has been speeded up. Steiner himself had grave doubts about the growing pace of technological development, warning his followers that materialist science gains its great power through unwittingly releasing Ahrimanic entities. In his last communications, Steiner called on his followers to develop their consciousness in order to rise above nature to the same extent that technology sank below it. He also gave a series of lectures about karma and its work in human history.

Steiner died on March 30, 1925. He had been ill for at least a year with an undisclosed stomach ailment, although there is some speculation that he had been poisoned. He continued lecturing until it was physically impossible for him to do so, and his followers were astounded when, on the evening of his last scheduled lecture, they found a note saying that it had to be canceled because of the Doctor's health. Nothing like this had ever happened before. The Doctor, they believed, was invulnerable. The exact nature of Steiner's illness remains unknown, but it is clear that his inability to refuse help to those who came to him was a key factor. Along with his public and private lectures and his practical work as a teacher, architect, and agriculturalist, Steiner made himself available to any who needed his counsel. For many years, he had practically no free time; and, wherever he went, his hotel room saw a constant stream of visitors including, on one occasion, Franz Kafka. Some asked about their astral bodies, others their diet or their marriages; Kafka asked about his writing. Steiner advised them all, giving little bits of himself to thousands. He was, as the Russian novelist Andrei Biely, a follower, once remarked, "a giant of the power of kindness." It is not hard to see how such solicitude would eventually wear anyone down.

In the end, it's difficult to give an exact assessment of a man whose work combines cogent criticisms of Kant with accounts of life in Atlantis. But this "mild, gentle, good, kindly man," whose achievement in "humanitarian terms is remarkable and enduring"—as the psychiatrist Anthony Storr wrote of Steiner in his study of gurus, *Feet of Clay*— remains, for devotees and non-initiates alike, something of an enigma.

Manly Palmer Hall: The Secret Teacher

You may not recognize the name, but Manly Palmer Hall (1901–1990) was one of the twentieth century's most prolific popularizers of all things mystical, esoteric, and occult. Along with writing more than fifty books on everything from astrology to the afterlife, for more than half a century Hall was the leading light behind the Philosophical Research Society, a spiritual organization devoted to promoting "ancient philosophy," whose fantastic Egyptian-Mayan styled headquarters still stands on Los Feliz Boulevard at the foot of the Hollywood Hills in Los Angeles. Here Hall lectured weekly to packed houses on dozens of arcane topics and maintained a unique collection of mystical objets d'art, famed among cognoscenti, and a library of rare alchemical and magical texts that attracted luminaries like C. G. Jung and Aldous Huxley. With his suave, leading-man looks, cultured manner, and rhetorical flare, Hall was a persuasive and inspiring speaker, and his influence and following spanned generations. Over the years, Hall's devotees included actors and actresses such as Bela Lugosi, Glenn Ford, Burl Ives, and Gloria Swanson; Hollywood bigwigs such as Sid Grauman, Cecil B. DeMille, and Samuel Goldwyn; politicians such as Harry S. Truman; scientists such as Luther Burbank; and other notables such as Elvis Presley, Sirhan Sirhan (Robert F. Kennedy's assassin), and the Apollo 14 moonwalker Edgar Mitchell.

Less known today than he was in the 1930s, '40s, and '50s, Hall made his name in 1928 with the publication of his encyclopedic *Secret Teachings of All Ages*, a remarkable compendium of Hermetic, Kabbalistic, Masonic, Rosicrucian, and generally obscure lore, which remains a treasure trove for researchers into all forms of arcana and still sells thousands of copies a year. The year 2008 marked the eightieth anniversary of the publication of this important work, but it also marked the release of the first biography of Hall, *Master of the Mysteries: The Life of Manly Palmer Hall* by Louis Sahagun. The coincidence—if that's what it is—of Sahagun's book appearing on the anniversary of Hall's masterwork seems significant enough to prompt a look at the strange life and even stranger death of one of California's most long-lived gurus.

Hall's career as a mystic sage began in 1919, when he came to California to be reunited with his mother. Both parents had abandoned their son at an early age—Hall never knew his father—and although he was born in Canada, Hall's early manhood has all the hallmarks of an archetypal American success story. He led a peripatetic childhood with his eccentric maternal grandmother, living in hotel rooms and train compartments, and was set for a career on Wall Street when her sudden death freed him from this path. Quitting his clerk's job, the eighteen-year-old left New York City; days later he exited the train in Los Angeles and headed for his mother's house in the sleepy Pacific coast community of Santa Monica. According to his biographer, Hall seemed to have had few hard feelings toward the mother who abandoned him, or at least he didn't mention them. Throughout his life Hall avoided confrontation with those close to him, preferring to acquiesce to their demands rather than risk an argument.

The California that Hall discovered was rife with "spirituality" and what we would call "New Age consciousness." In the early twentieth century, Theosophists, Freemasons, Vedantists, and Rosicrucians of varying authenticity prospered in the warm California sun. As one historian of new religious movements put it, "Hollywood is built on occult foundations." The fact that Sid Grauman, responsible for such

Hollywood landmarks as Grauman's Chinese Theatre, the El Capitan, and the very Hermetic Egyptian Theatre was, with Hall, a staunch Freemason, suggests this isn't an exaggeration. Young Manly haunted the amusement arcades on Santa Monica's beachfront, and one day was attracted by a sign advertising phrenology, the discipline that reads human psychology through the shape and contours of the skull. Intrigued by the diagrams of the brain and the anatomical charts he saw through the shop window, Hall went inside and asked the proprietor, Sydney J. Brownson, a Civil War veteran in his seventies, if he would like to "read his bumps." Brownson explained that phrenologists "make calculations by measuring the radial length of brain fibers from the pons of the medulla oblongata." Impressed, Hall listened as Brownson explained about magnetism, reincarnation, the aura, the wisdom of the ancients, the mysteries of India and the East, and the secret teachings of the church. Brownson quickly became Hall's guru, and his young student was entranced, eager to learn everything he could from the master.

Hall proved an excellent pupil, with a photographic memory and a talent for speaking, and a year later Brownson invited him to speak to a select audience who met weekly in a room above a bank. Hall was a success, his lecture on reincarnation dazzling the handful of elderly women who attended and rewarded the two with an offering of sixty-five cents, which the men quickly spent on chocolate sundaes. Thus Hall, who was an impressive six feet, four inches tall, began two activities that would last his lifetime: getting paid for speaking and indulging in sweets. Throughout his career, Hall maintained a secret life dedicated to binge-eating doughnuts; in later years, as he shunned exercise, his body grew to gargantuan proportions. The core message of his life's work, too, appeared at this time. For the next seventy years, in a variety of ways, Hall told his audiences that the universe was the creation of an invisible, living intelligence, and that in the remote past this truth had been hidden in the myths, symbols, and rituals of ancient societies. It was our task in the modern world to rediscover this secret and to benefit by it. It was a message that, in different ways, would be repeated by many others over the years.

Hall was so impressive a speaker that he was invited to address an audience at the Church of the People, one of Hollywood's most popular progressive religious forums. The lectures, held at the Blanchard Hall Building in downtown LA, were followed by lunch at Clifton's Cafeteria, a site later famous as the watering hole of the Los Angeles Fantasy and Science Fiction Society, whose members included L. Ron Hubbard, Robert Heinlein, and the Crowleyite rocket scientist, Jack Parsons. Hall became the church's main speaker, charging a dollar admission, an extravagant fee at the time. He also became the church's pastor and at nineteen was counseling men and women three times his age on the difficulties of life, becoming a "one stop source of an astonishing range of eclectic spiritual material."

But Hall wasn't alone; in a Hollywood filled with savants and swamis, he competed with other mystic seers. There were, for example, Princess Zoraida, "The Greatest Living Egyptian"; Pneumandros, "the Spirit Man"; Edwin J. Dwingle, founder of "Mentalphysics"; and the pyramidologist, "Professor" J. W. Parker, who claimed that the Great Pyramid of Egypt was "the Bible in stone." As today, when repackaged "secrets" of "mental science" top bestseller lists—witness the unsurprising success of *The Secret*—Hall's contemporaries blended mystic hokum with a get-rich-quick sensibility. But Hall wanted to be known as a philosopher and thinker, not merely a self-help huckster. He produced a series of pamphlets and newsletters like *The All-Seeing Eye*, spelling out his ideas on the spiritual and cultural future of America. His message reached important readers, some of whom made substantial financial contributions to his cause. One result was a trip around the world in order to study its sacred sites. Another was *The Secret Teachings of All Ages*, which Hall claimed was seven years in the making.

Described by Sahagun as a "gorgeous, dreamlike book of mysterious symbols, concise essays and colorful renderings of mythical beasts . . . and angelic beings," it appeared when Hall was just twenty-seven, and it made him nationally famous. It was an impressive tome. Weighing fourteen and a half pounds, between its thirteen- by nineteen-inch covers the reader found fifty-four original full color plates and two hundred black-and-white illustrations, and its double-columned fine font pages contained articulate essays drawing on more than six hundred sources. Seductively browsable, it remains a thrilling if not always reliable sourcebook on practically every aspect of the Western esoteric tradition. Selling at a hundred dollars a copy, its first two editions of eleven hundred copies sold out in advance, and further editions did equally well. For decades it was available only in its unwieldy "biblical" format—at the PRS Library today, a visitor's copy sits on an impressive lectern, and it's difficult to avoid thinking of the Ten Commandments. In recent years, however, a reader-friendly paperback has introduced the work to a new generation of seekers.

Hall's success made him a target for female Hollywood hopefuls wishing to share his mystic spotlight, if not his bed; for years Hall had promoted celibacy, and the tacit assumption was that any liaison with him would be sexless. But his sudden celebrity changed his mind, and it became known that Hall was looking for a real wife. While he could have had his choice of society women, in 1930 Hall married his secretary, Fay B. Ravenne, an attractive brunette astrologer from Texas. But the marriage soon proved difficult. Fay was subject to several illnesses—their exact nature is unknown—and she resented her husband's growing fame and success. In their decade together Hall's public star rose. Warner Brothers pumped him for film ideas, his library and art collection grew, and he traveled widely, befriending important people like the explorer Sir Francis Younghusband, the artist-mystic Nicholas Roerich, the mystical adventure writer Talbot Mundy, and the escape artist Harry Houdini. In 1934, he purchased a plot of land in Hollywood's Los Feliz district, near Griffith Park; here he planned to build the headquarters for his newly founded Philosophical Research Society, designing the "temple" in a fantastic "Atlantean" style. Troubled by fraudsters who preyed on naïve seekers, the public-spirited Hall received death threats after exposing a quasi-fascist self-help organization called Mankind United. Yet his home life (in a house built by the architect Frank Lloyd Wright) was disastrous. Hall suffered from numerous ailments, his relentless overeating his only relief from the misery of married life. Fay retreated deeper into depression; then, in 1941, she committed suicide, gassing herself in her car. Hall was devastated, but after a short period of mourning, he purged all record of Fay from his files, never mentioned her again, and got on with his career.

By 1944, America was at war, and Hall responded with patriotic fervor, his book *The Secret Destiny of America* promoting an esoteric version of Manifest Destiny that Bush-era theo-cons would have loved (one wonders if Hall was on their reading lists). Hall argued that the "seeds of democracy" had been planted on American soil millennia before the Christian era and that this "plan of the ancients" had been preserved through the centuries by secret societies, "pledged to condition America to its destiny for leadership in a free world." True or not, it was good propaganda in wartime, but one of Hall's readers took his idea and ran with it. In fact, she had already been running with it for some time. Marie Bauer, a petite German immigrant and mother of two, scoured Hall's writings and haunted his library, searching for confirmation of her own mystical-political insight. She was convinced that Sir Francis Bacon (who *really* was a Rosicrucian) had traveled to America, and while there had buried a vault beneath a church tower in Williamsburg, Virginia. In the vault were, Marie claimed, a fortune in gold, several unknown works of Shakespeare that proved he was really Bacon (Hall, too, accepted this idea), a plan to end war, and the location of similarly hidden vaults. God, Marie believed, had chosen her to uncover the vault; if she didn't, humanity was doomed. Her passion proved powerful enough to convince the proper authorities, and in the fall of 1938, Marie and her crew dug deep beneath Williamsburg's Bruton Parish Episcopal Church. Predictably, they found nothing; at least unbiased witnesses said the excavation was a failure. Marie thought otherwise and carried on, writing several books about the "Bruton vault" and its part in the coming "United Brotherhood of Earth." She did, however, give thought to her family, who were increasingly troubled by her bizarre behavior and her obsession with Hall, whose work, she believed, was of immense importance to her life purpose. The only fair thing to do, she concluded, was to get a divorce and abandon her children. After that, the next step was obvious. In December 1950, Hall and Marie were married. Her obsession with Bacon's vaults continued for the rest of her life, and at one point she was investigated by the FBI after she doggedly pestered every government agency she could think of to support her mission. This, along with her frequent hallucinations, fits of violence, and grandiose claims—at one point she bragged that she had mastered a means of controlling atomic energy—suggest that Marie was at least occasionally psychotic. Hall, it seems, tended to attract disturbed women.

By the 1950s, America's destiny as the protector and promoter of world democracy seemed secure, and an affluent society began to focus on other issues. From mystical insights into world politics, Hall's concern, and that of his audience, passed to health. Hall's own had always been shaky, and as other popular self-help programs like Dianetics promised miraculous results, Hall investigated a few eccentric approaches to alternative health. One was the work of the Hungarian émigré Edmond Bordeaux Szekely, cofounder of the International Biogenic Society, which was then operating out of Tecate, in Baja California. Szekely claimed to have a PhD from the University of Paris, to be fluent in ten languages, and to have developed a regime that promised "wholesome, meaningful, and spiritual fulfilment" through "nutrition, meditation, and self-analysis." Szekely based his ideas on a book he claimed to have translated from an Aramaic text, discovered in a secret archive in the Vatican. In his *Essene Gospel of Peace* (1936), Jesus apparently urges his followers to cleanse their "hinder parts" with an "angel of water," a kind of first-century colonics tool made from a gourd. Other of Szekely's works have an equal focus on the spiritual virtues of enemas. He also marketed a "biogenic battery" made of bound leaves of grass, which was to be brushed over the genitals. Whether this too was endorsed by Jesus is unclear.

Needless to say, the Aramaic text kept hidden by the Vatican existed only in Szekely's imagination, but the idea of being cleansed by an "angel of water" appealed to Hall, as did the regime of a strict fruit juice diet. In his last days, an updated "angel of water" was cleansing Hall twice daily, and its ministrations very likely contributed to his death in 1990, according to his family physician. By this time, however, Hall had come under the influence of an "alternative health expert" who hoped to capitalize on Szekely's dubious claims.

The 1960s and early '70s were a low point for Hall. Although the impressive headquarters, library, and lecture hall of the PRS was finally completed in 1959, and Hall, keeping his nose to the wind, augmented his discourses on ancient philosophy with insights into UFOs, by the mid-'60s it was clear that his rather conservative values were out of step with the Swinging Decade. His diatribes against the modern world, rock music, free love, hedonism, and drugs seemed the whining of a grumpy senior citizen, and indeed by this time Hall himself was in his sixties. Yet even in the threatening world of rock 'n' roll, Hall had followers. According to Larry Geller, Elvis's spiritual advisor in the '60s, the King once sent Priscilla to one of Hall's lectures so that she might develop an interest in the esoteric. Geller also claims that in the early '70s he bought a new deluxe edition of the *Secret Teachings* for Elvis at the PRS bookshop. When Hall overheard whom the copy was for, he signed it. Elvis reportedly asked Geller to tell "Mr. Hall how much I appreciate this."

By the late '70s, when I heard Hall speak at more than one of his Sunday morning lectures, the PRS had gained a new lease on life, rejuvenated by the burgeoning New Age movement and the new speakers its excellent facilities attracted. Stephan Hoeller, another Hungarian émigré and bishop of the Ecclesia Gnostica, a Gnostic church in Hollywood; Huston Smith, the MIT professor of religion and philosophy; Stanley Krippner, professor of psychology at the Saybrook Institute in San Francisco; the psychologist Bruno Bettelheim; Edgar Mitchell; and Willis Harman, of the Institute of Noetic Sciences, all became familiar speakers and fellow travelers of Hall's society. Others, like the "psychic archaeologist" Stephan Schwartz, also became closely involved with Hall.

While the new interest in metaphysics, spirituality, and a more holistic science found a welcome forum at the PRS, its own politics were in disarray. Its finances were a shambles, its files disorderly, maintenance minimal, security practically nonexistent. Hall's copyrights had lapsed, his priceless library wasn't even insured, and the building itself needed extensive repairs. The aging Hall had difficulty delegating authority and obliged assistants to facilitate his binges on sweets. Marie fluctuated between dictatorialness and evident dementia. And her imprudent boasts about the combined value of the PRS's and Hall's considerable assets attracted precisely the kind of spiritual con men he had battled in years gone by.

One of these was "Dr." Daniel Fritz, a 1980s adherent of Edmond Szekely's colonic philosophy. Among other beliefs, "Dr." Fritz—he had no real medical qualifications—claimed that giving birth near dolphins would ensure a highly evolved child. That many of the women taken in by this idea sued him after attending his clinic in Hawaii suggests just how feasible this practice was. However, Fritz, like most con men, was undeterred by setbacks, and at a New Age event in Santa Monica he wheedled his way into Marie's confidence. Although Manly was at first suspicious, for the less than savvy Marie, Fritz was a "godsend," and he quickly made himself indispensable to the pair, enjoying a dangerous intimacy with and access to both the Halls' and their society's wealth. Aged, ill, and at times confused, Hall's reluctance to confront associates gave Fritz almost carte blanche. An antique coin dealer who knew Hall grew suspicious when the "Doctor" presented several valuable coins claiming he was selling on Hall's behalf; when the dealer mentioned this to Hall, he merely said to "let it go." This was only one incident. Soon Fritz was helping himself daily to the several cookie jars left open by the increasingly senile Hall, and it wasn't long before the "Doctor" had the run of both the society and Hall's life.

Fritz became as much a fixture at the PRS as Hall, and as the latter's health grew increasingly fragile, the "Doctor" took charge of his treatment. For the most part this consisted of repeated doses of Szekely's "angel of water" combined with a rigorous fruit juice diet. As Dr. Sterling Pollack, Hall's family physician, later argued, this regime more than likely pushed Hall closer to his death, increasing his heart problems (brought on by his obesity) by depleting his electrolytes. Although Pollack repeatedly warned Hall of this danger, the philosopher found it impossible to refuse Fritz's treatments.

By this time Fritz was in charge of both Hall and Marie, blocking any direct access to them and vetting all contacts. Recognizing that Hall was more than likely heading for the afterlife, Fritz decided that he might as well make his control of both Hall's and the PRS's assets—valued then at around $5 million—official. There was, however, that problem of the will Hall had drawn up some years before, leaving everything to Marie and his stepchildren. Fritz's solution was to draw up a new will.

On August 23, 1990, Fritz impressed on Hall that he needed his signature on a document that would relieve him of any burdensome business regarding the many changes needed at the PRS. Hall, who had no idea what he was signing, was too tired and ill to resist and took the pen. Perhaps the "Doctor" even helped him move it across the page? In any case, it was done. Six days later, Fritz called Forest Lawn mortuary and Dr. Pollack to tell them that Hall had died peacefully in his sleep. When Pollack and the undertakers arrived to retrieve the body, they were stunned. Hall's pale, huge form lay on a creaseless bed, and out of his mouth, ears, and nose streamed thousands of ants. A cleaning crew was busy scrubbing out reddish-brown stains on the carpet, and Fritz and his son, who had also helped "care" for Hall, were carting his valuables out to their car. When Pollack asked where the ants came from, Fritz replied, "I don't know." Understandably suspicious, Pollack immediately canceled the death certificate he had written out. When asked what he was doing with Hall's belongings, Fritz mentioned the new will. It was the first Pollack had heard of it, and when he informed Marie, she finally twigged to what was going on.

Hall, Marie, Fritz, and his son are all dead, and the case remains, as Sahagun writes, "an open-ended unsolved Hollywood murder mystery" worthy of Raymond Chandler. When she realized that Fritz had pulled a fast one, Marie waged a tenacious legal battle against him, challenging the new will. She eventually regained control over most of Hall's personal assets, most of which she had to use to cover legal fees. The PRS, however, remained in Fritz's control, and cronies he had placed on its board of directors did all they could to keep the honey pot open. Botched autopsies, recalcitrant coroners, lack of decisive evidence, and standard bureaucracy impeded police attempts to nail Hall's murder on Fritz. But they were sure he did it. The ants—an Argentine variety, it turned out, after one was discovered stuck between Hall's teeth—could not possibly have been in Hall's home, an expert testified, and could only have entered Hall's body after death, and only outside in open country.

A second autopsy revealed several bruises, smudges of soil, and evidence of trauma on Hall's body and argued that Hall had asphyxiated face down in the dirt and hadn't died peacefully in bed. This could only have happened during the bizarre expeditions to Santa Barbara that Fritz insisted Manly and Marie make in a motor home owned by the PRS a week before. On two occasions the engine supposedly overheated, although there was no evidence of this, and Marie was advised to join Fritz's son, who was following them in a separate car, leaving Hall alone with Fritz. The first time she refused; miraculously, the trouble disappeared, and the motor home returned to LA. The next day the same thing happened. This time Fritz insisted Marie go on while he and Hall waited. This time she reluctantly agreed. She never saw her husband alive again. Police believe that while Marie went on to Santa Barbara, Fritz either left the severely fragile Hall to die of exposure in the hot California sun or helped him along. The ants, they believe, seeking water, would have been attracted to Hall's body fluids and entered him through various orifices while he was lying on the ground. The carpet stains were traces of soil. Weakened by his "angels of water," a severely ill Hall would not have lasted long in the Southern California heat.

Hall's end, bizarre and macabre as it was, shouldn't overshadow the significance of his early masterwork. *The Secret Teachings of All Ages* remains an indisputable classic. The PRS, under new management, remains a vital center for metaphysical investigation and in recent years received academic accreditation. And though not sparing of warts or skeletons in closets, Sahagun's gripping biography is an insightful look at the life and times of one of the last century's most important mystical thinkers.

CHAPTER NINE

Dion Fortune: Psychic Warrior

On Sunday mornings during the height of the Battle of Britain, several people could be found huddled together in 3 Queensborough Terrace, Bayswater, engaged in an activity most Londoners wouldn't have recognized as part of the war effort. Imagining themselves part of the "group soul of the race," these otherwise respectable citizens visualized "angelic Presences, red-robed and armed, patrolling the length and breadth of our land." Further meditations had them patrolling mine fields off the coast of Norway and performing astral commando raids on high-ranking Nazis. This magical effort against Hitler and Co. continued throughout the war, and although its effect on the dark forces of National Socialism may be doubted, the earnestness of those participating was unquestionable. The fact that during the Blitz not one but two German bombs fell on the headquarters of the Fraternity of Light—the group behind this spiritual resistance movement—might suggest that the Führer recognized the threat and tried to eradicate it. The further fact that those engaged in these etheric expeditions spoke of astral dogfights and mystical punch-ups might also suggest that there was more behind them than just patriotic wishful thinking.

The leader of this occult National Guard was at any rate very familiar with magical battles. In fact, it was through one such row itself that she first became involved in the occult. Having learned early on how to defend herself from psychic attack, and having devoted many years to mastering the mystic arts, by the time Hitler made a bid to annex Britain she undoubtedly felt capable of defending not only herself, but her nation. The name of this remarkable character was Dion Fortune, and she was one of the most brilliant figures of twentieth-century esotericism.

This, however, was not her name at birth, or at least not at her first one. The individual who took the name "Dion Fortune" at her second, magical birth was christened Violet Mary Firth and was born in Llandudno, North Wales, on December 6, 1890. As is true of many esoteric figures, little is known of Violet's early years; as one writer remarks, she "obscured the details of her life and the true nature of her personality behind a cloak of glamour and illusion," something that could be said of other occult figures, like Madame Blavatsky and Aleister Crowley. Her father came from the prosperous steelmaking Firth family of Sheffield. Arthur Firth didn't follow this line, becoming a solicitor, although by the time of Violet's birth, he was running the Craigside Hydropathic Establishment in Llandudno, having already run a similar spa-hotel in Bath—an apt career, perhaps, for the father of someone for whom the sea would be a central symbol of mystery, magic, and power.

Violet's mother, Sarah, was a Christian Scientist, and in her early years Violet, too, felt the impact of Mary Baker Eddy's ideas. But there were other, stranger experiences that presaged Violet's life to come. At the age of four, she began to have visions of a past life in Atlantis. She saw, she said, "pictures that formed themselves unbidden in the mind in that interval between the putting out of the nursery light and the oncoming of sleep"—what we would call hypnagogic hallucinations. She speaks of a "sandy foreshore" and a level plain, with great mountains rising sharply in the distance, of a river and strange trees that it wasn't safe to go near, of dangerous beasts in the river and equally dangerous people, of grassy vegetation, an indigo sky and a copper-colored sun. Were these images of an actual past life, or psychic postcards from the Jungian collective unconscious? Or were they the kind of fantasies an imaginative and lonely little girl might entertain herself with? Whatever the nature of these strange visions, they stayed with Violet throughout her life and led her to believe that her true home wasn't in a sleepy seaside resort, but in some lost world that she could return to only through her imagination. In later years, although she claimed that she wasn't "naturally psychic," Fortune would channel a remarkable work of occult metaphysics, *The Cosmic Doctrine*, which was "received" in 1923 but not published until 1949, after her death. This was her attempt at doing what Madame Blavatsky had done in *The Secret Doctrine*: reveal the hidden structure of the cosmos. Although *The Cosmic Doctrine* remains a difficult work and is generally read by serious devotees only, it suggests that the visions of some other life that haunted the young Violet were not mere preschool make-believe, but an early expression of her strange ability to enter and make herself at home in other worlds.

But although the young Violet had visions of prehistoric Atlantis, and at fourteen was writing poems about the sea, her real introduction to the mystic path came in her early twenties and in a drearily mundane context. When Violet turned twenty, her parents decided to enroll her in a residential college. The Studley Horticultural and Agricultural College is said to have offered places to "young ladies with slight emotional problems." From the little we know about Violet's teens, we get the impression of an imaginative, withdrawn, somewhat snobbish ("I have a constitutional repulsion for 'crushes,'" she wrote, "and give them scant politeness"), highly intelligent, and creative woman who, like many others, had to find a place for herself in the world. Violet would find her path at Studley, but not in the way she, or anyone else, might have imagined.

The Warden of Studley College was a pioneering female doctor named Lilias Anna Hamilton. She had traveled in Afghanistan—where she had been court physician to the emir—and India, where she had learned techniques of mental domination that made her a terror to the students. Violet had been at the school only a short time when the Warden asked her to give false evidence against an employee she had illegally fired. Violet was reluctant, but Hamilton's insistence and powers of persuasion overcame her scruples. Her method was to stare at Violet and simply repeat her commands; after the interview, Violet felt dazed and exhausted and slept for fifteen hours. Other incidents occurred, with Violet reluctantly complying, until the Warden turned her sights on an elderly woman, seeking control over her finances. Violet informed the woman of the scheme and hastily got her away and into the safekeeping of her relatives.

When Violet realized the Warden knew of her part in this rescue, she decided to leave the school before she herself fell victim to her powers. A fellow student who had felt Hamilton's wrath advised her to leave without seeing the Warden again. "You will not get away if you don't. I have tried several times and I cannot," she said. Violet was troubled by this advice but was determined to tell the Warden what she thought of her. When she did, Hamilton agreed to her leaving, but then adopted her Svengali pose and insisted: "You are incompetent and you know it. You have no self-confidence and you have to admit it." She repeated this mantra for the next four hours, with Violet transfixed and unable to break away. She knew that if she agreed with the Warden, her "nerve would be broken" and she would be useless in life. "By the time one realizes it that something abnormal" is going on, she wrote, one is more or less "glamoured" and "one cannot move or turn away." Eventually Violet heard a voice suggesting she pretend to accept the Warden's terms, otherwise she would end up like the girl who had warned her. She did, even going down on her knees to ask forgiveness. This satisfied the Warden, who let her go. Violet had entered the room a "strong and healthy girl" and left it a "mental and physical wreck." She stayed that way for three years.

Determined to understand what had happened, Violet began to study psychology. By this time she had moved to London and was taking classes in psychoanalysis at the University of London and had joined the Medico-Psychological Clinic in Brunswick Square; she may also have worked at the Tavistock Clinic. The Theosophical Society had recently started a club near Brunswick Square, and Violet started visiting, not because of a real interest in Theosophy, but because they offered cheap meals. As a Freudian, she dismissed Theosophists as cranks, but when, for fun, she attended a meditation class, something odd happened.

She saw a distinct image of a garden with blue flowers right before her eyes, rather like the hypnagogic images of Atlantis she saw as a child. When the instructor remarked that she had been trying to project the mental image of delphiniums, Violet realized that some kind of thought transference had happened. Earlier she had noticed that some of her patients seem to "drain" her of energy and that they even seemed to suck power out of electronic equipment. They acted, she thought, as some kind of vampire, something Freudian theory couldn't explain. She attended more lectures at the Theosophical Society and realized that Freud's ideas were too narrow. Something else was needed, and she soon found it.

Although Fortune's later work drew on psychoanalysis, producing what some have called a psychologized occultism, she dropped out of the clinic and, as World War I had begun, joined the Women's Land Army. Her time at Studley served her well, and she was put to work for the Food Production Department of the Ministry of Agriculture. Here she discovered a means of making milk from soybeans and even wrote a book about it, *The Soya Bean* (1925), but failed to capitalize on a discovery that could have made her rich. Her job for the Land Army required long hours of observing bacteria, and in the quiet stretches her vision turned inward. Again, something strange happened: her "astral sight" had opened, and the experience was disturbing. At the Theosophical Society she read Annie Besant's *The Ancient Wisdom* (1897). Much as Besant, a Fabian Socialist, had been converted after meeting Madame Blavatsky, Fortune was suddenly convinced of the reality of the Masters, superhuman beings who guided humanity in its evolution. For the next ten days, she entered a weird "astral" dimension, the experience culminating in a visitation by Jesus. Other Masters appeared—Melchizedek, "Lord of Flame and Mind"; Thomas Erskine, a Lord Chancellor in Dr. Johnson's time; Sir Thomas More—and in one vision they accepted her as a student.

With the end of the war, Violet left the Land Army. It was around this time that she met the Irish Freemason and occultist Theodore

William Moriarty, the model for her psychic detective in *The Secrets of Dr. Taverner* (1926), her collection of occult short stories. Violet joined the group of students, mostly women, who belonged to Moriarty's Science, Arts, and Crafts Society, and in the introduction to her Dr. Taverner stories, she writes that he was "the greatest mind I ever met" and that she owed "the greatest debt of my life" to him. "Without 'Dr. Taverner,'" she writes, "there would have been no Dion Fortune." Her *Cosmic Doctrine* is based on Moriarty's rare book *Aphorisms of Creation and Cosmic Principles* (1923). Moriarty himself died of angina pectoris under mysterious circumstances in a hotel in King's Lynn in August 1923, and Fortune was supposed to have received the messages from the inner planes that make up her book not long after his death. Some have suggested that Fortune simply took Moriarty's work and, after his death, "improved" on it. Whatever the truth, *The Cosmic Doctrine* remains a controversial work in several ways. The occult historian Francis King thought it had much value, while the occult artist and writer Ithell Colquhoun thought it was rubbish.

Strangely enough, *The Cosmic Doctrine* got Violet into trouble with her next magical group. While still studying with Moriarty, Violet renewed an old friendship with Maiya Curtis-Webb (later Maiya Tranchell-Hayes), a friend of the family. Maiya, like Moriarty, was an occultist, and she introduced Violet to the occult novelist J. W. Brodie-Innes, who was a member of the Hermetic Order of the Golden Dawn's Amen Ra Temple. The original Golden Dawn numbered W. B. Yeats and Aleister Crowley among its members, but by this time it had split into competing groups. In 1919, Violet Firth was initiated into the Golden Dawn, taking "*Deo, non fortuna*" ("by God, not by luck") as her magical motto; it was, as it happened, the Firth family motto as well. This soon morphed into Dion Fortune.

Another Golden Dawn temple was run by Moina Mathers, widow of S. L. MacGregor Mathers, one of the original group's leaders. Although at first friendly to Dion, even agreeing with her idea to start a more public occult group to attract more members (what would become the

Fraternity of the Inner Light), Moina soon developed a more critical attitude. What troubled her were the articles Dion had published in the *Occult Review*, which later became her book *Sane Occultism* (1929). Arguing that an "immense mass of verbiage has gathered around the Sacred Science since Madame Blavatsky drew back the curtain of the Sanctuary," and asking why occultism had produced "such a crop of charlatans and few, if any, intellects of the first water," Fortune's articles didn't win her many friends, and among those she angered was Moina Mathers. Mathers was also angry that in Fortune's early work *The Esoteric Philosophy of Love and Marriage* (1924), a book that dealt, however mutely, with the question of sex and the occult, she had revealed certain magical secrets that she had no right to communicate. Fortune sidestepped this when she argued that as she had yet to be introduced to these secrets—she was not yet of that grade—she couldn't very well reveal them. But the real reason behind the tension was that Fortune's energy, drive, and superior attitude rubbed many people the wrong way, and Moina, an older woman, felt threatened by her. It also can't have helped that Fortune had written that the Golden Dawn was being led by "widows and grey-bearded ancients." When Moina saw a rough draft of *The Cosmic Doctrine*, she declared that it was inconsistent with Golden Dawn teachings and added the trenchant criticism that "certain symbols had not appeared" in Fortune's aura. Moina gave Fortune an ultimatum: either forget her revelations and get back in line, or leave. Fortune left.

In *Psychic Self-Defense* (1930), Fortune describes an astral battle between herself and Moina Mathers. This time, however, she was no longer a "shy, vulnerable adolescent" but a "strong, magnetic leader." After writing of the "abuses prevalent in occult fraternities," Fortune received a letter warning her of the consequences if she continued her exposé. Believing her work was inspired by the Masters, Dion stuck to her guns. The result was a prolonged attack that only ended with an astral catfight between her and Moina.

Demon faces appeared, and Fortune and those around her suffered from a feline infestation: the headquarters of her Fraternity of Light and its neighbors were overrun by mobs of black cats. The place was filled with "the horrible stench of the brutes," and at their day-job offices, members of the group found "the same penetrating reek of the tom-cat." Astral cats appeared, too, and one morning after breakfast Fortune was confronted by "a giant tabby . . . twice the size of a tiger." The invasion ended after Fortune performed an exorcism, but she was soon grappling with her enemy anew. During an essential astral journey, Fortune encountered Moina, dressed in the robes of her grade. She refused Fortune right of way, and a battle ensued. Moina won the first round, throwing Fortune back into her body, which somersaulted over her followers, who had gathered in a vigil. Remembering her lesson with the Warden, Fortune got back on the astral plane and this time won the tussle. But that night she discovered that her back was covered with the scratch of a "gigantic cat." Later, Fortune also believed that Moina was responsible for the death of her friend Netta Fornario, an artist and occultist who was found dead on the Scottish isle of Iona. Her nude body was also found covered in scratches, lying in a ritual position on a cross cut into the turf. Moina, however, had been dead herself for eighteen months by the time Fornario, who seems to have been a depressed personality, apparently committed suicide. Fortune would no doubt have argued that committing murder from the afterlife would not have been beyond the powers or vindictiveness of her Hermetic nemesis.

The battle with Moina Mathers seemed to mark a new beginning for Fortune. Along with the house in Bayswater, she set up occult camp in Glastonbury, in a spot near Chalice Well and the Tor, in a house that was later bought by the writer Geoffrey Ashe. She had already met and worked with Bligh Bond, who had excavated the ruins of Glastonbury Abbey, supposedly with the help of the spirit of one of its deceased monks, and together they contacted inner entities she called "the Watchers of Avalon." Glastonbury became a symbol of the "mystical nationalism" that fueled her later anti-Nazi activities and expressed her aim to resuscitate the Western esoteric tradition, as opposed to Theosophy's very popular Eastern variants; it's no surprise that she left the Theosophical Society in 1927. Fortune thought much about race—too much for our tastes these days. She believed that the Western soul was unsuited for Eastern esoteric disciplines, and she wanted to provide access to our own homegrown spiritual traditions. In the decade that followed, she produced an impressive body of work, which included at least two classics. One is *The Mystical Qabalah* (1935), to my mind the most readable and straightforward exposition of the West's fundamental esoteric philosophy, in which she draws on the work of both MacGregor Mathers and Crowley. The other is perhaps her finest work in occult fiction, *The Sea Priestess* (1938), in which a humdrum estate agent's life is transformed by an affair with a modern-day priestess of Isis. At the time, Fortune had to self-publish it because witchcraft laws were still on the books in England, and the novel was considered too controversial by mainstream publishers. Many have come to an appreciation of the Western inner path through reading Fortune's fiction, and in novels like *The Demon Lover* (1927), *The Winged Bull* (1935), *The Goat-Foot God* (1936) and *Moon Magic* (1956)—her last book, whose final chapters were alleged to have been channeled—Fortune communicates in clear and evocative prose the essence of her spiritual vision.

The time also marked a change in her personal life. In 1927 she married Thomas Penry Evans, a Welsh physician, who had his own mystical path; Fortune called him "Merl" after Merlin. Although they shared magical pursuits, the two did not seem well matched. Fortune was a large, mannish, "Viking-like woman," and, like so many occultists—Madame Blavatsky, Crowley, Gurdjieff, Manly P. Hall—she put on weight in her later years. Evans was a small, dark Celt. Sex was never a major part of the union, nor even a minor one; again, like Madame Blavatsky, Fortune seemed to disdain it, although it runs as a magical current through her novels, and the discerning reader can chart the fortunes of her marriage in them. Fortune was the dominant and older partner, and accounts are that she bossed Evans constantly; the occultists Kenneth Grant and Israel Regardie both report that she henpecked him "unmercifully." Fortune seems to have overcompensated for her treatment at the Studley agricultural college; according to Grant, she grew "very partial to the idea of power" and "did not scruple to tell her followers how they should arrange their private lives." In 1939, Evans left her for a younger woman. The divorce was amicable.

In later years Fortune's work increasingly focused on trance mediumship and contacting the Masters on the inner planes. In the early 1930s, she leased a house near London's Belgrave Square called the Belfry, where she performed the rites of Isis that would find fictional expression in *Moon Magic*. Her following in the Fraternity grew and would eventually include such later magical authorities as W. E. Butler, W. G. Gray, and Gareth Knight.

When World War II broke out, Fortune turned her powers toward protecting the Sceptered Isle, whose spiritual tradition she had spent decades promulgating; and from Bayswater, Glastonbury, and other points in besieged Britain, she had her students radiate psychic energies, hoping to keep the dark forces at bay. Whether it was this effort or the work of a black magician in Hitler's inner circle who, she believed, directed baleful energies at her, the war years saw her health decline. Many who knew her in her last years said she was a "burnt out shell." One of these was the late Kenneth Grant, who said that when he met her in 1945, she "was close to death and had lost much of her physical force and vigor." Grant believed Fortune was "the magical Shakti of the New Age," linking her to Crowley's vision of a "new aeon"; and he describes some late meetings between Fortune and Crowley, a magician she had steered clear of in her early years. Apparently they corresponded, and Grant recalled a "stack of Crowley/Fortune letters" that allegedly met an unfortunate fate. After Crowley's death in 1947, the letters were sent to Karl Germer, then head of Crowley's Ordo Templi Orientis. Germer later moved to California and made the mistake of living near some of Charles Manson's Family. Some of the Family burgled his home and, among other items, took Crowley's letters. These were then lost in a fire started at the Family home by a disgruntled junior member. Whatever the truth of this tale, my suspicion is that, if the letters existed, they were probably no great esoteric loss: Crowley's letters are generally about himself, and his missives to Fortune would probably be of the same stamp. For researchers and biographers, of course, it's a different matter.

Toward the end, Fortune visited a Jungian analyst; she felt she was moving toward some great crisis in her life and needed guidance. She was obese, unkempt, alone, and surrounded by students of a dubious quality—a common fate for esoteric teachers. The analyst found much darkness in her dreams. She contracted blood poisoning from a badly extracted tooth, and it is unclear if it was this, or the leukemia she was diagnosed with, that killed her. On January 8, 1946, Dion Fortune passed through "the gates of death," as one of her posthumously published books is entitled. She was fifty-five and one of the last great occultists from the Golden Age of modern esotericism. Her influence continues today in various forms, inspiring Wicca, mystical feminism, and other movements. Marion Zimmer Bradley's bestseller *The Mists of Avalon* owes much, it is said, to Fortune. And her fraternity—now known as the Society of the Inner Light—carries on.

If Fortune started out wondering why occultism had produced "few intellects of the first water," a look at her career suggests that, in at least one instance, it had.

Aleister Crowley: The Beast Himself

M y first encounter with Aleister Crowley—self-styled Great Beast 666 and the most famous magician of the twentieth century—happened in 1975. I was nineteen and living in New York City, playing bass guitar in an underground rock band, and sharing a small one-bedroom flat in Little Italy with the lead singer and the guitarist. The guitarist had a kitschy interest in the occult, which manifested mostly in the pentagrams, upside-down crosses, and other satanic bric-a-brac that competed for wall space in the flat with old Velvet Underground posters and photographs of the Ramones. Squashed into a bookcase bursting with creased sci-fi and horror paperbacks were pummelled copies of Crowley's novels, *Moonchild* (1929) and *Diary of a Drug Fiend* (1922). I had already seen a copy of this last work in the window of the old St. Mark's Bookshop, and as drugs were something I, and practically everyone I knew at the time, was interested in, I looked forward to reading it.

Like tattered copies of the *I Ching*, Timothy Leary's *High Priest,* and *The Tibetan Book of the Dead*, Crowley's books were part of the debris left behind by the '60s generation. The Summer of Love had long since passed, but relics from that time still turned up amidst the fading tinsel of glam and the surfacing of what would in a year or so be christened punk. Certainly my attraction to Crowley at this stage wasn't unique, and when Chris—the guitarist—saw me turning the pages of the *Diary* he said something like, "Yeah, that book's cool. He's into coke, opium, everything." No doubt I said "cool" too, and went back to reading. This in itself tells us something about Crowley, which I suspect is still true today. Although he remains the most famous magician of modern times, Crowley's initial attraction for most people isn't his idiosyncratic, eclectic reading of the Western esoteric tradition—as intriguing as it is—but his extravagant, excessive lifestyle. Long before McDonald's, Crowley led a supersized life, running through an enormous amount of drugs, sex, and what we can call, for lack of a better word, "experience."

Crowley drank experience like champagne, and he never seemed to have enough of it, as a reading of his *Confessions of Aleister Crowley* (1969) or John Symonds' *The Great Beast* (1973)—still the most readable book on Crowley—will tell. He walked across China and climbed a Himalaya or two, learned several languages, and could easily have been a chess champion among other things, having enough adventures along the way to cover dozens of ordinary lives. Yet, after spending some years fascinated with the Great Beast—as he enjoyed being called—and reading practically everything he wrote (including the poetry), and practicing the magical disciplines he devised in order to accomplish the Great Work of the Knowledge and Conversation of the Holy Guardian Angel, I came away wondering if all the experience he absorbed actually did him any good. The virtue of experience is that it affects you in some way and *changes* who you are, which pretty much is what the Great Work is all about. (You may prefer to call it spiritual transformation, but the essence is the same). But what struck me after reading and rereading Crowley's work and the reports of his life, either by himself or by less biased hands, is that he never changed at all. For all the enormous helpings of life that he swallowed whole, and all the mystical disciplines he undoubtedly mastered, Crowley seemed the same self-centered, egotistical, and megalomaniacal person at the end of his life as when he started out. The *Tao Te Ching* observes that "the farther one travels, the less one knows." Among his many accomplishments, Crowley rendered his own version of this Taoist classic, yet he seems not to have grasped the wisdom of that insight.

I should also point out that the context for my introduction to the Great Beast was again not in any way esoteric. At the time I knew nothing about esotericism, magic, Kabbalah, or any mystical tradition. I was a rock 'n' roller. If I had heard about the Hermetic Order of the Golden Dawn, it was through the horror writer Arthur Machen by way of H. P. Lovecraft. Not many Manhattan proto-punkers were talking about Rudolf Steiner or Gurdjieff or Madame Blavatsky then. Crowley had been picked up by the last generation of rockers as a counterculture icon because of the wild sex, copious drugs, and general "bad boy" reputation—it had, I think, very little to do with magic—and this street-cred carried over to us. The Goths, death rockers, and heavy-metalers who discover Crowley today, do so, I think, for similar reasons, and it's a shame that many people get their first look at Western esotericism through his peculiar appropriation of it. Through my own experience, I know it takes an effort to shake that off. Crowley's philosophy of jettisoning all repression and inhibition and "going large" (he called it discovering your "True Will") appeals to youth, perennially hemmed in by parental and societal constraints and as yet lacking the power of discrimination and the virtue of self-discipline. But what is for most of us a stage in life we pass through on the way to (with any luck) maturity was for Crowley the "word of the Aeon." The age he saw inaugurated by his own hand was that of the "crowned and conquering child." Is it surprising that teenagers would be into it? Or that Crowley himself acted like a spoiled adolescent more times than not?

But although my first taste of *Crowleyanity* (as Crowley first thought of calling the religion he would unleash upon the world, before he opted for *Thelema)* was through the attraction of a good read about drugs, the result was something I hadn't expected. Not long afterward, we moved into one floor of a huge, illegal loft space on the Bowery, and one of the other denizens was a wild, flaming artist who was a devotee of Crowley's Thoth Tarot Deck, copies of which were rare at the time. He painted canvases based on the cards' images, and often he would do a reading for inspiration. By this time I had raced through *Moonchild*, Crowley's venomous roman à clef about the other members of the Golden Dawn, and had discovered Colin Wilson's *The Occult*, which had a long chapter on Crowley. The artist had other books too, like Israel Regardie's *The Tree of Life*. I read this and several others on "magick," as Crowley spelled it, and found that I was hooked. There was a kind of revival of occult literature at the time, and many cheap editions of occult classics by A. E. Waite, S. L. MacGregor Mathers, and others found their way to the remainder tables. The old Samuel Weiser occult bookshop was still around, and it had complete sets of reprints of Crowley's famous magical journal, *The Equinox*, going for practically nothing. I bought those and anything else that I could get my hands on having to do with magic(k), the occult, and specifically Crowley. I had read a great deal of Nietzsche by then, and his ideas about the *Übermensch* ("superman") seemed to chime with what Crowley was saying about the True Will. But Nietzsche, although a more profound thinker, had had a wretched life, got syphilis the one time he had sex, and didn't really talk about drugs. Crowley seemed a more promising role model. And, I had to admit, he looked pretty impressive in those photographs, with his black robe and hood, with the shining eye in the pyramid, performing the Banishing Ritual of the Pentagram, or as a turbaned Arab, enjoying his pipe of rum-soaked perique tobacco.

But my real plunge into the land of Do What Thou Wilt didn't happen until I moved to California. By the autumn of 1977 I had left the group and with my girlfriend had moved to Los Angeles, where I started my own band. Along with other sites that catered to occult tastes, here I haunted Gilbert's Bookshop on Hollywood Boulevard—sadly, long gone—which had been a favorite of Jimmy Page and David Bowie. One day I noticed a sign advertising a Crowley group. I answered it and a few weeks later was initiated into two of Crowley's magical societies. The Ordo Templi Orientis (Order of the Eastern Temple, or OTO) had been around since 1900, starting up in Germany in the early years of rising Aryan consciousness; Crowley became the head of an English branch in 1913. The Argenteum Astrum (Order of the Silver Star or A ∴ A ∴) emerged in 1907 after Crowley had fallen out with both the Golden Dawn and its head, MacGregor Mathers, and decided to start his own secret society. Although both groups had a Masonic, Rosicrucian flavor, the real core of the teaching was Crowley's inspired sacred text, *The Book of the Law* (1904), to which we owe his notorious call and response: "Do what thou wilt shall be the whole of the law. Love is the law, love under will."

Dictated to Crowley in 1904 in a Cairo hotel by the extrahuman intelligence Aiwass, *The Book of the Law* was, Crowley claimed, a sign that "the equinox of the gods had come, and that a new epoch in human history had begun." Crowley was convinced that the Secret Chiefs had chosen him as the new Messiah, and, although he balked at first, he soon took to the job with relish.

For several months I did what I wilt with zeal, upsetting my girlfriend by following the rituals Crowley provided at the back of his impenetrable 1929 work, *Magick in Theory and Practice*. (In *New York Rocker: My Life in the Blank Generation*, a memoir of my years as a musician, I give a fuller account of this time in my life.)

Yet, as I made my way through the rest of Crowley's oeuvre and became familiar with other works on magic and the Western spiritual tradition, my appreciation of the Master Therion (as he also styled himself, *therion* being Greek for "beast") began to shift. The people I had met through the Crowley group seemed to equate doing what they wilt with doing what they liked, which meant indulging in whatever appetites they cared to, along with a general lack of consideration for others. This led me, after a year or so, to drop out, although to this day I'm not quite sure how my membership stands. Initially I admired Crowley's enormous self-obsession (which makes his *Confessions* his most readable book; he is a great raconteur, especially about himself). But eventually it began to pall, and a kind of claustrophobia began to accompany reading his work. While he talked about philosophy, literature, and other pursuits that interested me, the punch line was always himself. This same inability to lose himself shows through in "visionary" works like *The Vision and the Voice* (1910) that, for all its angels and demons, still has Crowley's ego smack at the center, and it also colors *The Book of the Law*, which, for all its inspiration, reads like a combination of Oscar Wilde, Nietzsche, and the Marquis de Sade, with some Egyptian motifs thrown in. Crowley famously equated himself with Shakespeare, and although he is capable of insight, generally his remarks about other thinkers are made in order to justify his own colossal self-regard. Once, when disappointed by W. B. Yeats's lack of enthusiasm for his poetry, Crowley explained that Yeats simply couldn't admit that he, Crowley, was the better poet. A brief comparison of the two argues against this. Although works like the "Hymn to Pan" do have a strong incantatory power, most of Crowley's poetry is pretty insipid, even the pornographic works, which reveal a childish fascination with being "naughty," as do his slightly sick paintings on similar themes.

I also began to tire of Crowley's inexorable self-justifications, whether it was rationalizing his sadistic, slow murder of a cat when he was fourteen (in order, he said, to observe whether or not it really did have nine lives) or his (for any decent human being) inexcusable conduct during his ill-fated attempt to climb Kangchenjunga, the world's third-highest mountain. Crowley fell out with the other members of the expedition, and he refused to help when they met with an accident. His attitude was "serves them right," and several men died. He then withdrew all of the expedition's funds from the bank and justified himself in a spate of newspaper articles. Similar episodes crowd his turbulent and depressing life. Interestingly, it was only while mountaineering that Crowley experienced anything like a release from his ego and his constant itch to shock the bourgeoisie. He confessed that his "happiest moments were when I was alone on the mountains" and that "the moment the pressure was relieved, every touch of the abnormal was shed off instantly." He didn't even feel the need to write poetry, and the experience had nothing to do with magick.

But Crowley never outgrew his petulant spitefulness, a product, no doubt, of his childhood under fanatical Christian fundamentalist parents. But what was the point of discovering his True Will if it basically meant condoning these and other sociopathic acts? Did he really need the gods to OK his acting unforgivably? Crowley was incapable of recognizing that his actions affected other people and that he was accountable for them; in a way this suggests a kind of autism. His philosophy was a nihilistic Buddhism. "Let there be no difference made among you between any one thing & and any other thing," *The Book of the Law* declares. "The word of Sin is Restriction." Crowley recognized no restrictions, and if, as *The Book of the Law* revealed, there was no difference between one thing and another thing, what difference did it make if he did one thing or another? Which meant, of course, that he might as well do whatever he liked, as the universe condoned it anyway. A handy ethic, no doubt, but not one suited for any kind of spiritual growth. And in case any lingering sense of human sympathy managed to intrude, *The Book of the Law* was always there. "These are dead, these fellows; they feel not." "We have nothing with the outcast and the unfit; let them die in their misery." "Compassion is the vice of kings: stamp down the wretched & the weak." Much heavy weather has been made about Crowley's possible Nazi sympathies, and most of it is probably rubbish, but it isn't difficult to see the similarities between this kind of sensibility and the one that would have Europe in flames a few decades later.

Crowley's attitude to women is also notorious, but not surprising. When they were Scarlet Women, available for his sex magick, they were useful. Otherwise he had no time for them, and tragically, most of those who entered his life came to a bad end. Crowley abandoned Rose Kelly, his first wife, who helped him receive *The Book of the Law*, and their daughter, Lilith, in the middle of Asia; Lilith died soon after, and Rose later spent time in a mental asylum. Leah Hirsig, his most compatible Scarlet Woman, once allowed a goat to penetrate her during one of Crowley's rituals. The animal's throat was cut at the same time, and she also had the Beast eat her shit. She became a drug addict with Crowley and a prostitute after he dumped her. At least two other Scarlet Women went insane and one other committed suicide. Possibly the only creature Crowley ever loved was the daughter he had with Leah; sadly, she too died at his infamous Abbey of Thelema in Mussolini's Sicily.

"Intellectually . . . they did not exist," was Crowley's assessment of women, and "it was highly convenient that one's sexual relations should be with an animal." (Doubly convenient, then, for Leah and the goat.) Although such remarks, while objectionable, aren't rare even today, Crowley's lack of any real friendship even with his male followers again suggests a kind of autism. Once, when his most intelligent disciple, Israel Regardie, complained about some criticism Crowley made of his work, Crowley circulated a letter in which he accused Regardie of suffering from an inferiority complex, chronic constipation, and excessive masturbation, which was only relieved when he caught gonorrhea from a prostitute. Regardie recognized "the nasty, petty, vicious louse" that Crowley was on "the level of practical human relations," but his admiration for Crowley as a mystic enabled him to separate the man from the magus, an act of fission that Crowley apologists still perform today. But how to forgive the Beast for abandoning the mathematician and devout Thelemite Norman Mudd, who, shattered by Crowley's betrayal, filled his pockets with stones and drowned himself off the Isle of Guernsey? Or for the death of Raoul Loveday, at Crowley's Abbey, after drinking the blood of a sacrificed cat? Or for his sadistic treatment of the poet Victor Neuberg, with whom Crowley carried out an evocation of the demon Choronzon in North Africa, which included himself being sodomized? Or for the dozens of friends he left holding the bag or picking up the bill when he was faced with some difficulty or had dined at the most expensive place in town?

It's tempting to say that all these individuals were weak, neurotic personalities to begin with and that it isn't Crowley's fault that they were unsuccessful at life. But then why did he waste his time with them? Surely a man who once announced he had "crossed the Abyss" and become a god—which Crowley apparently did when he claimed he reached the magical grade of Ipsissimus in 1921—would find better things to do? The answer is that Crowley *liked* having neurotic people around him, because they were susceptible to his domineering personality. The relationships were dysfunctional: he enjoyed impressing his will on other people, and they enjoyed basking in the glow of his dominance and in having someone provide a purpose for their life, however dubious. It's instructive that Crowley had regard only for people he couldn't bully, like the mountaineer Oscar Eckenstein and the Buddhist Allan Bennett. And on one occasion when he encountered a personality stronger than his own—during his alleged visit to Gurdjieff's Fontainebleau Prieuré— the Beast apparently got a bit rattled.

One also has to admit that Crowley's last days, spent down-at-heel in a somber boardinghouse in Hastings, near the English Channel, were not encouraging. By the time he died at the age of seventy-two in 1947, Crowley was taking enough heroin each day to kill a roomful of nonusers. He had spent the better part of a lifetime doing what he willed, but his final years were full of boredom and regret and pitted with the pains of poverty and ill health.

The drugs were understandable and, if excessive, were not unusual. The sex, too, was obsessive, and we all know people who take advantage of the weak-willed on occasion. And I do owe Crowley a debt of gratitude for introducing me to a canon of literature—the Western esoteric tradition—the study of which has become for me a lifelong pursuit. I hasten to emphasize here that I haven't once made a criticism of magic or the occult, but of Crowley the man. I almost want to say, "If only he had used his powers for good instead of evil." But that would be wrong. Crowley wasn't really evil, just insensitive, selfish, and oblivious to anything except his own raging ego, and getting over *that* strikes me as the first hurdle in any initiation. I think he was a serious student of magick and really did have some insights into tapping the little-known powers of the will. But that's no excuse, and I've no doubt that, more times than not, he really was a beast.

Julius Evola: Mussolini's Mystic

In the late spring of 1980, Italians felt the return of a terrorist threat that for the previous decade had kept a low profile. Since the end of World War II and the rise of the cold war, neofascism had been a fact of life in Italian politics, the right-wing ideals of "tradition" and "order" seeming the only alternative to American domination or the threat of communism. In December 1969, the destabilizing tactics employed by the neofascists reached a new height with the Piazza Fontana bombing in Milan, a violent spark that ignited a wave of far-right terrorism. By the mid-1970s, however, the neofascist threat appeared to have faded, only to be replaced by its left-wing opposite when radical groups took to shattering university professors' kneecaps for teaching the doctrines of "the establishment."

Their counterparts, however, were merely lying low, and on May 28, 1980, it was clear that they were back and ready for action. On that day, an Italian policeman, Franco Evangelista—nicknamed "Serpico" after the legendary New York cop for his success in arresting drug dealers—was assassinated by right-wing terrorists in Rome. Then, in June, a judge who had led an investigation into right-wing terrorist activities was murdered. But the major attack came last, on August 2, when a bomb in the Bologna railway station killed eighty-five people and wounded hundreds more. Many of the victims, including children, were maimed horribly. Like the Omagh bombing in Northern Ireland and 9/11, the event punched a hole in the nation's psyche—which was precisely what its authors intended.

Keeping to its "strategy of tension," the group responsible for the blast kept its identity secret, yet the police had a good idea who to look for. Names were mentioned: Paolo Signorelli, Franco Frela, Claudio Mutti, Stefano delle Chiaie, and others from the right-wing usual suspects list were questioned. And when the investigation began to close in, several members of the Nuclei Armati Rivoluzionari, an influential far-right group, fled the country for Britain. One man, however, whose name was mentioned by all, had no need to fear the police, as he had been dead for the last six years. But if a single person could be held accountable for the Bologna bombing, the dead man was a good candidate. His name was Giulio Cesare Andrea Evola, better known to his more recent English-speaking readers as Baron Julius Evola, author of several books on magic, esotericism, and the occult as well as a withering attack of Western civilization, *Revolt against the Modern World* (1934).

Born on May 19, 1898, to a noble Sicilian family, Julius Evola was a bright but self-willed child who rebelled early on against his strict Catholic upbringing. This resentment against Christianity remained with him throughout his life and fueled a Nietzschean disdain for the weak and ignorant masses. Although he left university before earning a degree, from his studies in industrial engineering he developed a sense of precision and objectivity, a cold clarity and logic. But it was the new movements in modern literature that had the most influence on Evola's early years. In later life he was to become a staunch defender of tradition, but in his teens Evola came under the spell of the literary avant-garde, absorbing the work of writers like Giovanni Papini and Giuseppe Prezzolini. Papini introduced him to new ideas in art and fashion, as well as to the writings of Meister Eckhart and several oriental sages. But the most influential discovery was the work of Filippo Tommaso Marinetti, whose Futurist movement would later find favor with Italy's Fascist dictator, Benito Mussolini, a position Evola himself would occupy in years to come. Marinetti, who sang the praises of the modernity Evola would eventually come to despise, may seem an unlikely mentor for a philosopher whose polemics against the modern world would later guide several violent attacks on it. Yet Marinetti's own fascistic sensibility—a virulent rejection of nature, a celebration of regimen and machinelike efficiency, and above all an embrace of speed and violence for their own sake—are in keeping with Evola's character.

Marinetti's Futurists scandalized the bourgeoisie with their penchant for avant-garde hooliganism and artistic thuggery, starting fights at art galleries and shouting abuse at poetry readings, tactics that less cultured individuals would later employ against a variety of human targets. War, for Marinetti, was an aesthetic affair, and his reports from the Turkish front in World War I spoke of the "joy" of hearing "the machine guns screaming a breathlessness under the stings slaps *traak-traak* whips *pic-pac-pum-tum*. . . . " These and other brutal onomatopoeia informed Marinetti's ideas of *parole in libertà*, "free words," which later formed the basis of much of today's rap and performance poetry.

At nineteen, Evola had an opportunity to test Marinetti's theory when he joined the Italian army in the last days of the war. Although serving as an artillery officer at the Austrian front, Evola saw no action, yet the discipline, order, and hierarchy of the military impressed him and left him unsuited for civilian life, with its muddling chaos and growing egalitarianism. It was then that he began his search for transcendence, first through drugs, then through a study of the occult.

These experiences seemed only to increase Evola's sense of purposelessness, and the idea of suicide came to dominate his consciousness, a morbid opinion made attractive through his interest in the brilliant but disturbed Austrian writer Otto Weininger. The Jewish Weininger wrote an influential book, *Sex and Character* (1903), in which he argued that man alone is a spiritual creature, yearning for the celestial heights, while woman, a denizen of the earth, tries to trap him in her corrupting embrace: the archetype of the femme fatale. He also argued that the Jews as a race displayed distinctly "feminine" characteristics, most importantly a hatred of all things of a "higher" nature: hence Marx and his reduction of religion to the "opium of the people." An unhappy individual, obsessed with sex and his own Jewishness, Weininger committed suicide at twenty-three, in a room in Vienna once occupied by Beethoven. His ideas about women and Jews, however, lived on in several minds, not the least of which was Evola's.

A Buddhist text saved Evola from suicide, and the discovery of a new avant-garde movement gave him a sense of direction. Futurism, he came to believe, was vulgar and showy. But Dada, the new anti-art movement seeping across the border from Switzerland, struck him as more intellectual as well as more ambitious. Dada seemed more than a mere art movement, something along the lines of a total reconstruction of the world, the need for which Evola had come to believe in passionately. It is also quite possible that in Dada's leader, Tristan Tzara, Evola found a new role model: photographs of Evola displaying his elegant, smooth, shaved face, immaculate dress, and imperious gaze—complete with monocle—are strikingly similar to those of Tzara. For the later advocate of tradition this is ironic, as Tzara, with his hunger for notoriety and scandal, would today more than likely be at home on talk shows and Twitter than in the workshops of anti-art.

Evola plunged into Dada, reading his poetry to the music of Schoenberg, Satie, and Bartok at the Cabaret Grotte dell'Augusteo, Rome's version of Zürich's infamous Cabaret Voltaire. He also took up painting and exhibited his work in Rome, Milan, Lausanne, and Berlin; today his *Inner Landscape at 10:30 a.m.* still hangs in Rome's National Gallery of Modern Art. Evola also wrote an influential essay on abstract art, arguing that it is only in abstraction that the existence of an "eternal self" could be expressed—an indication, again, of his anti-natural, anti-earthly bias.

Yet Dada was not enough. Disgusted with the increasing commercialization of the avant-garde, in 1922 Evola abandoned painting and poetry. He now gave himself to philosophy, writing several books of an idealistic character in which he spelled out the metaphysics of the "absolute individual." This boiled down to the doctrine that such an individual enjoyed "the ability to be unconditionally whatever he wants," and that for him "the world is my representation." For the nobly born Evola, this spiritual solipsism seems appropriate: it provided an ontological underpinning for his nearly absolute lack of interest in other people.

This focus on the "unconditional" freedom of the self led to a still deeper study of occultism. Evola became involved with an Italian Theosophical group and wrote an introduction to a translation of the *Tao Te Ching*. A correspondence with Sir John Woodroffe—writing as Arthur Avalon, author of several works on Hindu philosophy—led to a fascination with Tantra, which surfaced in Evola's books *The Yoga of Power* (1949) and *The Metaphysics of Sex* (1958): the latter also shows the influence of Weininger. Evola soon lost interest in Theosophy, but not in the occult, and by the mid-1920s he had become involved in an esoteric society, the UR group, which looked at magic as "the science of the ego." Formed around the occultist Arturo Reghini, editor of two influential occult journals, *Atanòr* and *Ignis*, the UR group embarked on a variety of esoteric investigations. Along with Tantra, Evola studied alchemy, Taoism, and Buddhism. The link between these studies was the idea of "initiation," the sense that through them Evola was participating in ancient initiatory practices, living manifestations of a lost primal tradition.

Yet he soon felt the need for something more than study and ritual. Linking his vision of Dada as an attempt to refashion the world to his new pursuits, Evola saw in politics and society a means of expressing his occult beliefs. He was impressed with Nietzsche's vision of a coming world nihilism, and later translated Oswald Spengler's bestselling study of cultural decay, *The Decline of the West* (1918–1923), into Italian. Mussolini's Fascism was, Evola believed, an attempt to introduce elements of a traditional culture into a corrupt modern world. What it lacked was a spiritual basis. Evola saw himself as the means of supplying this. The UR group took to performing magical rituals with the intent of inspiring the new Fascist movement with the spirit of ancient Rome.

On a more concrete level, Evola and his colleagues published a journal, *La Torre*, to which he contributed a series of political articles. Although he celebrated Mussolini's attempts to revive the ancient Roman Empire (at the expense of the Ethiopians), Evola argued that Fascism was too involved with the church and too ready to pander to the masses. It needed, he said, to anchor itself in a "spiritual aristocracy," an argument made clear in his book *Pagan Imperialism* (1928). Here Evola attacked Christianity and heaped scorn on both American democracy and the Soviet regime.

Mussolini was impressed with Evola's thought and was interested enough to write an article about it for Reghini. In the world of realpolitik, however, Mussolini knew that in Catholic Italy he had little chance of success without the church. It was his refusal to alienate the pope, as well as his shrewd manipulation of the masses, that eventually lost him Evola's sympathies. Evola never joined the Fascist party, a fact that years later served him in good stead, and although his political beliefs are at best questionable, one must at least admire his determination to stand by his own values. It would have been easy to secure a comfortable niche in the Fascist hierarchy. Yet Evola's criticism of Mussolini was unequivocal: after being told that Il Duce disagreed with something he had written, Evola replied, "*Tanto peggio per Mussolini*"—"Too bad for Mussolini." Yet after ten issues, *La Torre* had to stop publishing, and for a time Evola said he had to employ bodyguards. Later Mussolini softened and embraced some of Evola's less politically intransigent ideas.

A more powerful influence on Evola by this time was the French orientalist René Guénon, through whose forbidding books on metaphysics, esotericism, and tradition Evola found a formidable exponent of his own basic vision. Like Evola, Guénon had been brought up Catholic. Yet after studying philosophy he plunged into the world of fin de siècle occultism, and for a time was attracted to Theosophy and Freemasonry. He soon abandoned these for Hindu philosophy, through which he had discovered an insight into the ontological structure of the universe. This, he believed, had been intuited by the ancients, who had codified this knowledge in the form of a "primordial tradition." Although remnants of this primal truth could be found in the great religions, it was lost to the vast mass of humanity. The modern world was, in fact, caught in its own death throes, a product of the last stages of the Kali Yuga, the Dark Age that the West has been subject to for the last six thousand years. Guénon marshaled his argument in a short but incisive work, *The Crisis of the Modern World* (1927). Evola followed suit and brought out his own incendiary polemic seven years later.

Revolt against the Modern World must stand as one of the fiercest attacks on Western civilization ever written; I wouldn't be surprised if it was among the bedside reading of today's "traditionalist terrorists." (For what it's worth, although Evola remained partial to Hinduism, Guénon converted to Islam and spent his last years in Cairo.) A massive work, its two parts are divided into an account of what the ancient traditional world was like and an unremitting assault of the evils of modernity. Like many out of sympathy with secular society, Evola found no redeeming value in liberalism, democracy, humanism, or science. Toward the end of his life, when fledging neofascists sat at his feet seeking guidance and insight, Evola boiled the essence of his daunting tome down to a provocative and deadly epigram. "It is not a question of contesting and polemicizing," he told them, "but of blowing up everything." In Bologna in 1980, at least some of his readers took him at his word.

The argument of *Revolt against the Modern World*, if we can call it that, is lengthy and complex, but there is really very little argument in any philosophical sense. For the most part, Evola engages in an imperious declamation of his insights into tradition. His central insight is what he calls "the doctrine of the two natures." The world of tradition, he tells us, is based on the reality of an eternal truth, what he calls "being," which lies outside of time. The modern secular world, however, is one of "becoming," the messy, inchoate, ever-changing stream of nature and history. The distinction is a classic one, first posited by the Presocratic thinker Parmenides centuries before Plato, and has occupied philosophers ever since. Yet how Evola arrives at an entire civilization based on it is unclear. He scorns historians who labor over facts and evidence. Such busywork is outside tradition and so "unreal." Evola, on the contrary, achieves his insights through having attained a "superindividual and non-human perspective." Having done so, he eschews "debating and 'demonstration.'" "The truths that may reveal the world of Tradition," he tells us, "are not those that can be 'learned' or 'discussed': either they are or they are not." For Evola, evidently, they are, and he's managed to secure his knowledge by becoming "free of the obstacles represented by various human constructions," such as specialized historical research and reasoned argument. "Human constructions," he tells us, are to be avoided, as the truth of tradition can only be divined from a nonhuman perspective. The point is debatable, but whatever one may think of his "truths," the present writer has no difficulty finding some of them nonhuman.

For someone looking at the book today, it's difficult to think that the most important people taken with it at the time, Mussolini's Fascists and Hitler's Nazis (understandably, its mass appeal was nil), were less impressed by Evola's aristocratic disdain for argument—according to Evola, a distinctly Jewish pastime—than by his championing of a rigid social hierarchy, the belief in the supremacy of the noble Aryan race, and the glorification of the ruthless warrior. The Nazis had already drawn on some homegrown savants in this regard, pulling Nietzsche's remarks about a "good war that hallows any cause" and "the blond beast" out of context. (Unlike Evola, Nietzsche did see military action in the Franco-Prussian War; the experience made him a lifelong anti-militarist, and when the Nazi hacks cottoned to this, they gently shunted him to the side. The fact that he also vigorously rejected anti-Semitism didn't help.) But Evola built an entire sociology around the idea of the Kshatriya, the "holy warrior" of the ancient Hindu caste system, based on the Laws of Manu. Christianity, democracy, and humanitarianism were cancers eating away at the noble pagan soul, and the militaristic regimes of Mussolini and Hitler were a profound attempt to rejuvenate the race. Or at least part of it. In Evola's cosmic history, the noble Aryan people originated in the bleak but bracing realms of the North Pole, in the legendary land of Hyperborea ("beyond the north wind"). These manly types, exemplars of what Evola calls "virile spirituality," worshipped a solar god, "lived dangerously" in a static hierarchical system in which everyone knew his place, and enjoyed the beauty and vigor of a Golden Age, before the rot set in. This started when a catastrophic shift in the earth's axis led to a mass migration of the Hyperboreans, an exodus from their Arctic paradise into less bracing climes. Adopting some of Madame Blavatsky's ideas, Evola argued that his Arctic warriors migrated to North America and Siberia, then gradually down to the now-lost continent of Atlantis. At this point some of these Atlanteans mixed with an aboriginal southern race—possibly the Lemurians. These southern types were a different breed: nature-oriented, they worshipped an Earth Goddess, were peaceful, and lived in collective communities characterized by egalitarianism and sharing. They were also responsible for all the character traits that Evola and his friends found nauseating.

Gradually, through the cyclical nature of history, the Hyperborean virtues were eroded. As the world passed through its inevitable descent, the southern, feminine traits became predominant, housed specifically in various racial types like the Jew, until now, having passed through three previous *yugas* (ages), we've hit rock bottom with the decadent democracies of the West. (The clincher, apparently, was the Renaissance and the rise of humanism.) The fact that we are in the last phase of the Kali Yuga was, Evola believed, actually cause for celebration, as it meant that it had nearly come full circle, with a new Golden Age about to be born. All that was needed was a little help, and this, evidently, was where Benito and Adolf came in.

Although *Revolt against the Modern World* was published to practically no public notice (the German nationalist writer Gottfried Benn was one of the few to review it), the idea of a vast historical support for the supremacy of an Aryan warrior type caught on with the right people. Evola was once again in Mussolini's good graces and wrote extensively for a number of Fascist newspapers. He also wrote two influential books, *Aspects of the Jewish Problem* (1936) and *Outline of a Racist Education* (1941), and gave lectures on his racial ideas to university students. Less crude than the Nazi racial doctrines, which he found altogether too materialistic and biological, Evola argued that race was really a spiritual question. This meant, in effect, that one might be Jewish by birth but still harbor an Aryan soul; likewise, a "true-blooded" Aryan could be possessed by a Semitic spirit. (This, to some extent, explained how a lazy, undisciplined people like the Italians—at least to the average National Socialist's eye—could have descended from the Romans and could be able to participate in the glorious Aryan struggle.) Fastidious, cultured, and at bottom influenced by his profound study of esotericism, Evola found the Nazi racial idea vulgar and tried to pass on to them some of his own insights, once again attempting to put into practice his beliefs about tradition. He lectured to SS study groups and at the University of Berlin, and he was courted by Heinrich Himmler, who treated him to a tour of SS castles. Several of his books were translated into German, and he addressed influential gatherings, like Berlin's elite Herrenklub. This cachet had great effect at home; in 1938, when Mussolini enacted his own race laws, he used Evola as his guide. Three years later, in 1941, in an attempt to present himself as more than Hitler's puppet, Il Duce told the baron that his book *The Synthesis of Racial Doctrine* (1941) was the one the Fascists needed.

Evola's supporters cite his subtle thinking on the race question as evidence that he was never really anti-Semitic, but it's difficult to square this claim with his pronouncements that the Jews were "the anti-race par excellence," nor with the fact that he argued for the authenticity of the notoriously spurious *Protocols of the Elders of Zion*, with its ludicrous "evidence" of a Jewish conspiracy for world domination. He was also less than subtle in his response to the murder of his friend Corneliu Codreanu, the leader of the fascistic Romanian Iron Guard, who numbered the religious historian Mircea Eliade among its members. When he heard the news, Evola spoke of the "Judaic horde" and hurled invective against the "filthiest tyranny, the Talmudic, Israelite tyranny."

At different times his rhetoric also included denunciations of "inferior, non-European races," "Negro syncopation," and "sexual tormentresses" who had the audacity to wiggle their hips in very tight pants.

Evola's attempt to influence Nazi doctrine was unsuccessful: the Nazis weren't interested in Aryan Jews or vice versa, and in any case the difficulties in telling which from which were probably insurmountable. And although he made many German contacts, the pragmatic Himmler finally saw no use for him. Being rejected by Himmler may be a mitigating factor, but it hardly exonerates Evola for his ideas about race. It's difficult to think that his "spiritual racism" could have saved many Jews but easy to imagine that some "spiritual undesirables" might have met a sorry end.

Although he was the first person at Hitler's Rastenburg HQ to greet Il Duce after his daring rescue from prison in 1943, Evola's contact with the Nazis convinced him that Mussolini was second-rate. Evola briefly became involved with the short-lived Fascist republic of Salò, but he soon left Italy for Austria. Here, in 1945, during the blistering Soviet siege of Vienna, he was wounded in an air raid and left with both legs paralyzed, a handicap the spiritual warrior had to live with for the rest of his life. After the war, he returned to Italy, his hopes of a revival of tradition, courtesy of the Axis powers, profoundly dashed.

Yet his belief in occult politics remained. During the 1950s, Evola wrote about the "legionary spirit" and the "warrior ethic," but the triumphant tone of his earlier work had shifted. He called on *l'uomo differenziato*—"those who are different"—to drag their feet against the pull of democracy and materialism. A 1951 edition of *Revolt against the Modern World* no longer spoke of the heroic efforts of international Fascism and instead advised a philosophy of stoic resistance.

However, Evola's polemics aroused the authorities and he was summoned to court, accused of trying to revive Fascism. The fact that he had never joined the party—oversight or shrewd calculation?—as well as his eloquent defense cleared him of the charge, and in his book *Men among the Ruins* (1953) he outlined the need for a counterrevolution.

Yet age and the times were against him; in his last work, *Ride the Tiger* (1961), a meditation on how the believers in tradition could survive the final days of the Kali Yuga, Evola advocated *"apolitia,"* an "active nihilism." There was little hope, he said, of salvaging anything of value; all that was left to *l'uomo differenziato* was aristocratic disdain and the more visceral expedients of violence.

Ironically, it was the radical leftism of the 1960s that revived interest in Evola, and in the midst of the social, sexual, and psychedelic revolutions of that decade he was rediscovered by disaffected right-wing Italian youth who, strangely enough, linked his work to that of their other hero, J. R. R. Tolkien. Dubbed "our Marcuse" by his new devotees—a nod to the reigning doyen of leftist ideology, Herbert Marcuse—by the early '70s, half-paralyzed and grimly pessimistic, Evola held forth to wide-eyed young neofascists who absorbed his invectives against the intolerable modern world, along with reminiscences of Hitler, Himmler, and Il Duce.

"Nothing in this system deserves to be saved," he told them, and, by all accounts, they seemed to have taken this to heart. Some of those who frequented the stuffy rooms in his palazzo on Corso Vittorio Emanuele in Rome later carried on the baron's struggle to make the world safe for "virile spirituality"—some by writing far-right tirades themselves, others by courageously blowing up innocent people.

After Evola's death and his posthumous notoriety, his ideas reached the English-speaking world via the members of the Nuclei Armati Rivoluzionari who fled Italy after the Bologna bombing. Reaching England, they made contact with the right-wing National Front, whose younger members absorbed Evola's exciting new doctrines. By the late 1980s, his ideas had spread to wider audiences via the New Right magazine *The Scorpion.* By the 1990s, his ideas on spirituality, anti-modernism, and tradition found a place in the New Age movement, and by 1998 Inner Traditions, a major US esoteric publisher, had brought out English translations of many of his works. Perhaps the most ironic new advocates of Evola's ideas can be found in the darker side of hard rock. Starting in the late 1980s, a collection of goth, heavy metal, "black metal," and "industrial" groups embraced much of Evola's ethos, blending it with a heady cocktail of other influences. Marilyn Manson, Blood Axis, Non, Throbbing Gristle, and other "transgressive" acts found inspiration in figures such as Charles Manson, the high priest of the Church of Satan Anton LaVey, the dark magician Aleister Crowley, and Aryan ideology and fascist aesthetics, among other things. Michael Moynihan, coauthor of *Lords of Chaos*, a controversial account of far-right and neofascist Scandinavian black metal rock groups, is also a serious esoteric scholar and has edited an English translation of Evola's *Men among the Ruins* as well as an anthology of writings from the UR Group, *Introduction to Magic*; both are published by Inner Traditions. What's ironic about this is not that these groups should be attracted to Evola's ideas—they are, in their eyes, highly transgressive, and as such perpetually attractive to youth—but that any society that actually put them into practice would more than likely eliminate them and other advocates of "Reich and roll" as cultural undesirables.

Ultimately, there is a real danger connected with Evola's thinking: not his obvious Fascism or racism, but the fact that his writings are not merely the ravings of a lunatic. His prose is vigorous, intelligent, and often insightful, if uncongenial. Moreover, the modern world has thrown up some very real problems, and the materialism and spiritual poverty of the West have given rise to some very unwelcome responses. It may be an understatement, but human beings should be motivated by something more than consumerism and the dubious cachet of having "fuck" misspelled on your clothes. A hierarchical society based on racial superiority and a warrior breed is not, perhaps, the answer. But if history tells us anything, it's that if moderate individuals don't come up with a better idea soon, the resulting ideological gap will be filled by the less moderate among us. Current admirers of Julius Evola, I suspect, are banking on history repeating itself.

Jung and the Occult

On February 11, 1944, Carl Gustav Jung—then sixty-eight and the world's most renowned living psychologist—slipped on some ice and broke his fibula. Ten days later, in hospital, he suffered a myocardial infarction caused by embolisms from his immobilized leg. Treated with oxygen and camphor, Jung lost consciousness and entered what seems a near-death and out-of-body experience—or, depending on your perspective, delirium. Jung found himself floating a thousand miles above the earth. Seas and continents shimmered in blue light, and Jung could make out the Arabian desert and snow-tipped Himalayas. Jung felt he was about to leave orbit, but then, turning to the south, a huge black monolith came into view. It was a kind of temple, and at the entrance Jung saw a Hindu sitting in a lotus position. Within, innumerable candles flickered, and Jung felt that the "whole phantasmagoria of earthly existence" was being stripped away. It wasn't pleasant, and what remained was an "essential Jung," a core of his experiences.

Jung knew that inside the temple he would meet the people to whom he really belonged. The mystery of his existence, of his purpose in life, would be answered. Jung was about to cross the threshold when, from below, rising up from Europe, he saw the image of his doctor in the archetypal form of the king of Kos, the site of the temple of Asclepius, the Greek god of medicine. He told Jung that his departure was premature; many, most of them women, were demanding his return —and he was there to ferry him back. When Jung heard this, he was immensely disappointed, and almost immediately the vision ended. Jung experienced the reluctance to live that many who have been "brought back" encounter, but what troubled Jung most was seeing his doctor in his archetypal form. He knew this meant that the doctor had sacrificed his life to save Jung's. Jung tried to explain, but his doctor no doubt thought he was still delirious. On April 4, 1944—a date numerologists can delight in—Jung sat up in bed for the first time since his heart attack. On the same day, Jung's doctor came down with septicemia and took to his bed. He never left it and died a few days later.

Jung's visions continued. He thought his Swiss nurse was an old Jewish woman and that he was performing a Kabbalistic ritual, a mystic marriage of Tiphereth and Malkuth, sephiroth of the Tree of Life. Jung was convinced that he hadn't simply hallucinated, but that he had been granted a vision of reality. He had passed outside time, and the experience had had a palpable effect on him. For one thing, the depression and pessimism that had overcome him during World War II vanished. But there was something more. For most of his long career, Jung had impressed upon his colleagues, friends, and reading public that he was, above all else, a scientist. He was *not*, he repeated almost like a mantra, a mystic, occultist, or visionary, terms of abuse his critics, who rejected his claims to science, had used against him. Now, having returned from orbiting earth on the brink of death, Jung seemed content to let the scientist in him take a back seat for the remaining seventeen years of his life. (He died in 1961.)

Although Jung had *always* believed in the reality of the "other" world, he had taken care not to speak too openly about this belief. Now, after his visions, he seemed less reticent. Jung had, it seems, a kind of conversion experience, and the sort of interests the world-famous psychologist had until then kept to himself now became common knowledge. Flying saucers, astrology, parapsychology, alchemy, even predictions of a coming new Age of Aquarius: pronouncements on all of these dubious subjects—at least from the point of view of modern science—flowed from Jung's pen, so many that one critic dubbed him a "journalists' oracle." If Jung had spent a career fighting off charges of mysticism and occultism initially triggered by his break with Freud in

1912, by the late 1940s he seems to have decided to stop. The "sage of Küsnacht" and "Hexenmeister of Zürich," as Jung was known in the last decade of his life, had arrived.

Yet Jung's involvement with the occult was with him from the start—literally, it was in his DNA. Jung's maternal grandfather, the Reverend Samuel Preiswerk, who learned Hebrew because he believed it was spoken in heaven, accepted the reality of spirits and kept a chair in his study for the ghost of his deceased first wife, who often came to visit him. Jung's mother, Emilie, was employed by Samuel to shoo away the dead who distracted him while he was working on his sermons. She herself developed mediumistic powers in her late teens. At the age of twenty she fell into a coma for thirty-six hours; when her forehead was touched with a red-hot poker she awoke, speaking in tongues and prophesizing. Emilie continued to enter trance states throughout her life, when she would communicate with the dead. She also seems to have been a split personality. Jung occasionally heard her speaking to herself in a voice he soon recognized was not her own, at least not the voice she normally used. Emilie's remarks then were profound and expressed with an unexpected authority. This "other" voice had inklings of a world far stranger than the one that young Carl knew.

This "split" that Jung had seen in his mother would later appear in himself. At around the age of twelve, Jung literally became two people. There was his ordinary twelve-year-old self, and *someone else*. The "Other," as Carl called him, was a figure from the eighteenth century, a masterful character who wore a white wig and buckled shoes, drove an impressive carriage, and held young Carl, who was somewhat inept, in contempt. It's difficult to escape the impression that in some ways Jung felt he *was* this character in a past life. Seeing an ancient green carriage, Jung felt that it came from *his* time. Jung's later notion of the collective unconscious, that psychic reservoir of symbols and images that he believed we inherit at birth, is in a sense a form of reincarnation, and Jung himself believed in some form of an afterlife. Soon after the death of his father in 1896, when Jung was twenty-one, he had two dreams in which his father appeared so vividly that he considered the possibility of life after death. In another, later dream, Jung's father asked him for marital advice, as he wanted to prepare for his wife's arrival. Jung took this as a premonition, and his mother died soon after. And years later, when his sister Gertrude died—a decade before his own near-death experience—Jung wrote that "what happens after death is so unspeakably glorious that our imagination and feelings do not suffice to form even an approximate conception of it."

Jung's mother was involved in at least two well-known paranormal experiences that are recounted in practically every book on Jung. Sitting in his room studying, he suddenly heard a loud bang coming from the dining room. He rushed in and found his mother startled. The round walnut table had cracked from the edge past the center. The split didn't follow any joint, but had passed through solid wood. Drying wood couldn't account for it; the table was seventy years old, and it was a humid day. Jung thought, "There certainly are curious accidents." As if she was reading his mind, Emilie replied in her "other" voice, "Yes, yes, that means something." Two weeks later came a second incident. Returning home in the evening, Jung found an excited household. An hour earlier there had been another loud crack, this time coming from a large sideboard. No one had any idea what had produced it. Jung inspected the sideboard, then looked inside. In a cupboard where they kept the bread, Jung found a loaf and the bread knife. The knife had shattered into several pieces, all neatly arranged in the breadbasket. The knife had been used for tea, but no one had touched it or opened the cupboard since. When Jung took the knife to a cutler, he said that there was no fault in the steel and that someone must have broken it on purpose; it was the only way he could account for it. Jung kept the shattered knife for the rest of his life, and years later he sent a photograph of it to the psychical researcher J. B. Rhine.

By this time Jung, like many others, was interested in spiritualism and reading through the literature—books by Zöllner, Crookes, Carl du Prel, Swedenborg, and Justinus Kerner's classic, *The Seeress of*

Prevorst. At the Zofingia debating society at the University of Basel, he gave lectures on "The Value of Speculative Research" and "On the Limits of Exact Science," in which he questioned the dominant materialist paradigm that still reigns today. Jung led fellow students in various occult experiments, yet when he spoke to them about his ideas, or lectured them about the need to take them seriously, he met with resistance. Apparently he had greater luck with his dachshund, which he felt understood him better and could feel supernatural presences himself.

Another who seemed to feel supernatural presences was Jung's cousin Helene Preiswerk. In a letter to J. B. Rhine about the shattered bread knife, Jung refers to Helly—as she was known—as a "young woman with marked mediumistic faculties" whom he had met around the time of the incident; and in his posthumous autobiography, *Memories, Dreams, Reflections* (1963), he remarks that he became involved in a series of séances with his relatives *after* the incidents of the bread knife and table. Yet the séances had been going on for some time *before* the two events, and their center of attention was Helly, whom Jung already knew well and who, by all accounts, was in love with him. This is an early sign of Jung's somewhat ambiguous relationship with the occult.

Helly came from Jung's mother's side of the family. She would enter a trance and fall to the floor, breathing deeply, and speaking in old Samuel Preiswerk's voice, although she had never heard him speak. She told the others that they should pray for her elder sister Bertha, who, she said, had just given birth to a black child. Bertha, who was living in Brazil, had already had one child with her half-caste husband, and gave birth to another on the same day as the séance. Further séances proved equally startling. At one point Samuel Preiswerk and Carl Jung, Sr.— Jung's paternal grandfather—who had disliked each other while alive, reached a new accord in the afterlife. A warning came for another sister, who was also expecting a child. She would lose it, the medium said, although her grandfather tried to help her. In August the baby was born premature and dead.

At other séances Helly reached more feverish states. Her sister worried for her health, so they stopped. One reason for stopping may have been that Helly was using the séances as a means of getting Jung's attention. Helly began to utter messages that were surprisingly similar to those in *The Seeress of Prevorst*, which Jung had given her for her birthday, and her reliability became shaky. At later séances— they started again because Jung's mother felt the split table was a "sign" from Samuel—Helly produced another array of voices, but the most interesting was a spirit named Ivenes, who called herself the *real* Helene Preiswerk. This character was much more mature, confident, and intelligent than Helly, whom Jung described as absent-minded and not particularly intelligent, talented, or educated. It was as if buried beneath the unremarkable teenager was a fuller, more commanding personality, like Jung's "Other." This was an insight into the psyche that would inform Jung's later theory of individuation, the process of "becoming who you are." Helly did blossom later, becoming a successful dressmaker in France, although she died young, at only thirty.

In Jung's dissertation on the séances, *On the Psychology and Pathology of So-Called Occult Phenomena* (1903), he describes Helly unflatteringly as "exhibiting slightly rachitic skull formation" and "somewhat pale facial color," and he fails to mention that she is his cousin. He also omits his own participation in the séances and dates them from 1899 to 1900, when they had started years before. Jung's biographer Gerhard Wehr politely suggests that "the doctoral candidate was obviously at pains to conceal his own role, and especially his close kinship relationship, thus forestalling from the start any further critical inquiry that might have thrown the scientific validity of the entire work into question." In plain English, this means that Jung the scientist thought it a good career move to obscure Jung the occultist's personal involvement in the business.

In 1900 the twenty-five-year-old Jung joined the prestigious Burghölzli Mental Clinic in Zürich. Here he did solid work in word-association tests, developed his theory of "complexes," and initiated a successful patient-friendly approach to working with psychotics and schizophrenics. It was during his tenure here that he also became involved with Freud. From 1906, when they started corresponding, to 1912, when the friendship ruptured, Jung was a staunch supporter of Freud's work and promoted it unstintingly. There were, however, some rocky patches. One centered on the famous poltergeist in Freud's bookcase. Visiting Freud in Vienna in 1909, Jung asked him about his attitude toward parapsychology. Freud was skeptical and dismissed the subject as nonsense. Jung disagreed, and, sitting across from the master, he began to feel his diaphragm glow, as if it was becoming red-hot. Suddenly a loud bang came from a bookcase. Both jumped up, and Jung said to Freud, "There, that is an example of a so-called catalytic exteriorization phenomenon!" (Jung's long-winded circumlocution for a poltergeist, or "noisy spirit"). When Freud said "Bosh!" Jung predicted that another bang would immediately happen. It did. Jung said that from that moment on, Freud grew mistrustful of him, and that his look made him feel he had done something against him.

From Freud's letter to Jung about the incident, one gets the feeling that he felt Jung himself was responsible for it. This isn't surprising; Jung *did* manifest paranormal abilities. While in bed in a hotel room after giving a lecture, he experienced the suicide of a patient who had a strong transference on him. The patient had relapsed into depression and shot himself in the head. Jung awoke in his hotel, feeling an odd pain in his forehead. He later discovered that his patient had shot himself precisely where Jung felt the pain, at the same time Jung woke up. More to the point, a visitor to Jung's home once remarked about Jung's "exteriorized libido," how "when there was an important idea that was not yet quite conscious, the furniture and woodwork all over the house creaked and snapped."

It was Jung's break with Freud that led to his own "descent into the unconscious," a disturbing trip down the psyche's rabbit hole from which he gathered the insights about the collective unconscious that would form his own school of analytical psychology. He had entered a "creative illness" and was unsure if he was going mad. In October

1913, not long after the split, Jung had, depending on your perspective, either a vision or a hallucination. On a train he suddenly saw a flood covering Europe between the North Sea and the Alps. When it reached Switzerland, the mountains rose to protect his homeland, but in the waves Jung saw floating debris and bodies. Then the water turned to blood. The vision lasted an hour and seems to have been a dream that had *invaded* Jung's waking consciousness. Having spent more than a decade treating mental patients who suffered from precisely this kind of complaint, Jung had reason to be concerned. He was ironically relieved the next summer when World War I broke out and he realized his vision had been a premonition of it. Yet the psychic tension continued, and at one point Jung felt he would no longer fight off the sense of madness and decided to *let go*. When he did, he landed in an eerie, subterranean world where he met strange intelligences that lived in his mind. The experience was so upsetting that for a time Jung slept with a loaded pistol by his bed, ready to blow his brains out if the stress became too great.

In his recently published *Red Book* (2009), Jung kept an account, in words and images, of the *objective, independent* entities he encountered during his "creative illness"—entities that had nothing to do with Jung personally, but who *shared* his interior world. There was Elijah and Salome, two figures from the Bible who were accompanied by a snake. There was also a figure called Philemon, who became a kind of inner guru and whom Jung painted as a bald, white-bearded old man with bull's horns and the wings of a kingfisher; as a friend pointed out to me, Philemon bears an odd resemblance to Freud. One morning, after painting the figure, while taking a walk Jung came upon a dead kingfisher. The birds were rare in Zürich, and Jung had never before come upon a dead one. This was one of the many synchronicities—"meaningful coincidences"—that happened at this time. There were others. In 1916, still in the grip of his crisis, Jung again felt that something *within* wanted to get out. An eerie restlessness filled his home. Jung felt the presence of the dead, and his children did, too. One daughter saw a strange white figure; another had her blankets snatched from her at night. His son drew a picture of a fisherman he had seen in a dream: a flaming chimney rose from the fisherman's head, and a devil flew through the air, cursing the fisherman for stealing his fish. Jung had yet to mention Philemon the kingfisher to anyone. Then, one afternoon, the doorbell rang loudly, but no one was there. Jung asked, "What in the world is this?" The voices of the dead answered, "We have come back from Jerusalem, where we found not what we sought," the beginning of Jung's strange *Seven Sermons to the Dead*, a work of "spiritual dictation"—also known as channeling—that he attributed to "Basilides in Alexandria, the City where the East toucheth the West."

By 1919 World War I was over and Jung's crisis had passed, although he continued to practice what he called "active imagination," a kind of waking dreaming, the results of which he recorded in *The Red Book*. But spirits of a more traditional kind were not lacking. He was invited to London to lecture on "The Psychological Foundations of the Belief in Spirits" to the Society for Psychical Research. Jung told the SPR that ghosts and materializations were "unconscious projections." "I have repeatedly observed," Jung said, "the telepathic effects of unconscious complexes, and also a number of parapsychic phenomena, but in all this I see no proof whatever of the existence of real spirits, and until such proof is forthcoming I must regard this whole territory as an appendix of psychology."

Scientific enough, no doubt, but a year later, again in England, Jung encountered a somewhat more real ghost. He spent some weekends in a cottage in Aylesbury outside of London rented by Maurice Nicoll (later a student of Gurdjieff and P. D. Ouspensky), and while there was serenaded by eerie sounds as an unpleasant smell filled the bedroom. Locals said the place was haunted, and one particularly bad night, Jung discovered an old woman's head on the pillow next to his; half of her face was missing. Jung leaped out of bed and waited until morning in an armchair. The house was later torn down.

One would think that having already encountered the dead on their return from Jerusalem, Jung wouldn't be shaken by a fairly standard English ghost, but the experience rattled him. Yet his account of it only appeared thirty years later, in 1949, in an obscure anthology of ghost stories. When his lecture for the SPR was reprinted in the *Collected Works* in 1947, Jung added a footnote, explaining that he no longer felt as certain as he did in 1919 that apparitions were explicable through psychology and that he doubted "whether an exclusively psychological approach can do justice to the phenomena." In a later postscript he again admitted that his earlier explanation was insufficient, but that he couldn't agree on the reality of spirits, because he had no experience of them, conveniently forgetting the haunting in Aylesbury. But in a letter of 1946 to Fritz Kunkel, a psychotherapist, Jung admits that "metapsychic phenomena could be explained better by the hypothesis of spirits than by the qualities and peculiarities of the unconscious."

A similar ambiguity surrounds Jung's experience with the *I Ching*, the ancient Chinese oracle, which he began to experiment with in the early 1920s and which, like horoscopes, became part of his therapeutic practice. Although Jung mentioned the *I Ching* here and there in his writing, it wasn't until 1949, again nearly thirty years later, in his introduction to the classic Wilhelm-Baynes translation, that he admitted outright to using it himself. And although he tried to explain the *I Ching's* efficacy through what would become his paranormal deus ex machina, synchronicity, Jung admits that the source of the oracle's insights are the "spiritual agencies" that form the "living soul of the book," a remark at odds with his quasi-scientific explanation. Ironically, his major work on "meaningful coincidence," *Synchronicity: An Acausal Connecting Principle* (1952), written with the physicist Wolfgang Pauli, provides only one unambiguous example of the phenomenon, and readers like me, who accept the reality of synchronicity, come away slightly baffled by Jung's attempt to account for it by means of archetypes, quantum physics, statistical analysis, mathematics, J. B. Rhine's experiments with

ESP, astrology, telepathy, precognition, and other paranormal abilities, all of which read like a recrudescence of Jung's "I am a scientist" reflex. In the 1920s, Jung plunged into a study of the Gnostics—whom he had encountered as early as 1912—and alchemy, and it was he more than anyone else who salvaged the ancient Hermetic pursuit from intellectual oblivion. Another Hermetic practice he followed was astrology, which he began to study seriously around the time of his break with Freud. Jung informed his inner circle that casting horoscopes was part of his therapeutic practice, but it was during the dark days of World War II that he recognized a wider application. In 1940, in a letter to H. G. Baynes, Jung speaks of a vision he had in 1918 in which he saw "fire falling like rain from heaven and consuming the cities of Germany." Jung felt that 1940 was the crucial year "when we approach the meridian of the first star in Aquarius." It was, he said, "the premonitory earthquake of the New Age." Jung was familiar with the precession of the equinoxes, the apparent backward movement of the sun through the signs of the zodiac. By acting as a backdrop to sunrise at the vernal equinox, each sign gives its name to an "age"—called a "Platonic month"—which lasts roughly 2150 years. In his strange book *Aion* (1951), Jung argues that the individuation of Western civilization as a whole follows the path of the Platonic months and presents a kind of "precession of the archetypes." Fish symbolism surrounds Christ because Christ was the central symbol of the Age of Pisces, the astrological sign of the fish. Previous ages, of Taurus and Aries, produced bull and ram symbolism. The coming age is that of Aquarius, the water-bearer. In conversation with Margaret Ostrowski-Sachs, a friend of the writer Hermann Hesse, Jung admitted that he had kept this "secret knowledge" to himself for years and only finally made it public in *Aion*. Jung wasn't sure he was "allowed" to, but during his illness he received "confirmation" that he should.

Although the scholar of arcana Gerald Massey and the French esotericist Paul Le Cour had earlier spoken of a coming Age of Aquarius, Jung was certainly the most prestigious mainstream figure to do so, and it is through him that the idea became a mainstay of the counterculture of the 1960s and '70s. This was mostly through his comments about it in his book *Flying Saucers: A Modern Myth of Things Seen in the Sky* (1958), in which Jung argued that UFOs were basically mandalas from outer space. During his crisis, Jung had come upon the image of the mandala, the Sanskrit "magic circle," as a symbol of psychic wholeness, and he suggested that flying saucers were mass archetypal projections formed by the psychic tension produced by the Cold War that was heating up between Russia and America. The Western world, he argued, was having a nervous breakdown, and UFOs were a way of relieving the stress.

Jung wrote prophetically:

> My conscience as a psychiatrist bids me fulfil my duty and prepare those few who will hear me for coming events which are in accord with the end of an era. . . . As we know from ancient Egyptian history, they are symptoms of psychic changes that always appear at the end of one Platonic month and at the beginning of another. They are, it seems, changes in the constellation of the psychic dominants, of the archetypes or "Gods" as they used to be called, which bring about . . . long-lasting transformations of the collective psyche. This transformation started . . . in the transition of the Age of Taurus to that of Aries, and then from Aries to Pisces, whose beginning coincides with the rise of Christianity. We are now nearing that great change . . . when the spring-point enters Aquarius.

Ten years later the Fifth Dimension (whose name suggests the cosmic character of the Mystic Sixties) had a hit song from the hippie musical *Hair* echoing Jung's ideas, and millions of people all over the world believed it was "the dawning of the Age of Aquarius."

Jung died just on the cusp of the occult revival of the 1960s, a renaissance of magical thinking that he did much to bring about. He was also directly responsible for the "journey to the East" that many took then and continue to take today. Along with the *I Ching*, Jung gave his imprimatur to such arcane items as *The Tibetan Book of the Dead*,

Taoism, Zen, and other forms of the wisdom of the East, without which it is debatable if these Eastern imports would have had the popularity they had. That Jung was in many ways a founding father of the Love Generation is seen by his inclusion on the cover of the Beatles' *Sgt. Pepper's Lonely Hearts Club Band* album (1967), a work that more or less ushered in the age of pop psychedelia, although Jung himself would have thought flower power sadly naïve. Although for all his efforts Jung has never been accepted by mainstream intellectuals, his effect on popular culture has been immense, and our contemporary grass roots, inner-directed spirituality has Jung's name written all over it. Jung himself may have been equivocal about his relationship with mysticism, magic, and the occult, but the millions of people today who pay attention to their dreams, notice strange coincidences, and consult the *I Ching* have the old sage of Küsnacht to thank for it.

Chapter Thirteen

Ouspensky in London

For Russian intellectuals not partial to the Bolshevik revolution, 1919 wasn't exactly a good year. The earthquakes of anarchy brought on by a world war and then a civil war, and the prospect of an unknown and uncertain future, sent artists and thinkers suspicious of Lenin and the Bolsheviks running to Europe. Berlin, Paris, and London swelled with the influx of émigrés. And for esoteric philosophers, obsessed with questions of time, consciousness, and the "psychology of man's possible evolution," it may have seemed a particularly inauspicious year.

Such might have been the feeling of P. D. Ouspensky, philosopher of the eternal recurrence, author of a work on translogical metaphysics, and, at the time, a somewhat beleaguered student of the enigmatic Greco-Armenian teacher, G. I. Gurdjieff.

In chapter eighteen of his masterpiece, *In Search of the Miraculous* (1949), the story of his time with Gurdjieff, Ouspensky tells of his escape from the revolution and of his journey across Russia, from St. Petersburg through the Caucasus, to Turkey, Constantinople, and the outskirts of Europe. The record reads like an adventure story. Russia at that time had become a vast minefield of war, famine, sickness, and crime, and Ouspensky's report rivals the less than verifiable accounts of Gurdjieff's own spiritual journeys in *Meetings with Remarkable Men* (1963). As a journalist, Ouspensky covered the revolution in a series of letters for the *New Age*, the London magazine of ideas edited by the man who would soon take Ouspensky's place as Gurdjieff's chief lieutenant, A. R. Orage.

Ouspensky's account of everyday life during the revolution, his analysis of political events, and his profound antipathy for the Bolsheviks come through in his *Letters from Russia: 1919.* They flesh out the cool, distant, philosophical voice characteristic of *In Search of the Miraculous.* Times were difficult. In one letter he writes: "I personally am still alive only because my boots and trousers and other articles of clothing—all 'old campaigners'—are still holding together. When they end their existence, I shall evidently end mine."

While the workers of the world united, the author of books on the Tarot, the fourth dimension, and the superman, whose talks about India and his travels in the East filled lecture halls in St. Petersburg and Moscow, carried luggage as a house porter to support his family.

But in 1919 Ouspensky experienced more than a physical journey and revolution. As the charismatic "arch-disturber of sleep" Gurdjieff led his band of students across an exploding Russia, Ouspensky faced his growing doubts about his teacher and decided to act. Since 1915, when they first met in a cheap Moscow café, Ouspensky had sat at Gurdjieff's feet and absorbed his teaching. The irony of meeting the "magician" Gurdjieff in precisely the drab, gray, everyday world that Ouspensky had journeyed to the East in order to escape was not lost on his commentators—nor, I think, on Ouspensky himself.

At the start of his inner and outer adventures with Gurdjieff, which would eventually lead him to London and independent work, Ouspensky said that he "had come to the conclusion a long time ago that there was no escape from the labyrinth of contradictions in which we live except by an entirely new road, unlike anything hitherto known or used by us." He knew then as "an undoubted fact that beyond the thin film of false reality there existed another reality from which, for some reason, something separated us."

The "miraculous" that he searched for was a penetration into this new reality. That he should find it in an unfashionable back-street café, frequented by small dealers and commission agents, and not in the ashrams of India or the bamboo jungles of Ceylon, must have piqued his sense of the absurd. Subsequent events could only have added to it, not the least of them his uncertainty about Gurdjieff as a transmitter of what Ouspensky later came to call the "system."

As any practitioner of Gurdjieff's Fourth Way soon discovers, a mystery theater atmosphere surrounds the lives of its early advocates. Some see the split between guru and chela as a vast historical symbol, a living hieroglyph of esoteric wisdom, acted out by Gurdjieff and Ouspensky for some reason unknown to their followers and perhaps unknowable except for some future students. Others see Ouspensky as a weak intellectual, unable to grasp the true import of Gurdjieff's teachings; see, for example, James Moore's less than unbiased account in *Gurdjieff: The Anatomy of a Myth* (1991) and William Patrick Patterson's *Struggle of the Magicians* (1997). Still others, like me, simply recognize that however remarkable a man Gurdjieff was, Ouspensky himself was no pushover. The mind capable of writing *A New Model of the Universe* (1931) would sooner or later leave Gurdjieff's nest and set up on his own.

And such, at the beginning of his perilous escape from the revolution, were Ouspensky's own thoughts. During a six-week stay in Essentuki, in the Caucasus, Gurdjieff, according to Ouspensky, began to change. Suddenly, for no reason, he abandoned the "work on themselves" he had put his followers through for the previous three years and said he was leaving for the Black Sea. Why had he stopped, especially after the great difficulties his group had faced in getting the "work" started there? Ouspensky "had to confess that my confidence in G. began to waver from this moment." Thus began a separation that cost the philosopher many a painful decision and a trial by fire that at times had the potential of costing him his life.

It is clear from his letters that Ouspensky loathed his time in Ekaterinodar, a city of squalor, bribery, and sickness. He came there by way of Essentuki, where he had arrived at his momentous decision to leave Gurdjieff. It was not a sudden revelation, but the product of a slow, cumulative process. "For a whole year," he writes, "something had been accumulating and I gradually began to see that there were many things I could not understand and that I had to go."

And so he tried. When conditions got worse—with Cossack raids on the Bolshevik-occupied city—Ouspensky decided to leave. He would try to reach London, where he knew Orage and others from the *New Age* and where he could make a living with his pen. But he wouldn't leave before Gurdjieff. Reluctant to abandon his teacher, Ouspensky stayed until the last moment, waiting until Gurdjieff left before making his own departure.

But by then it was too late. Madness erupted, and Ouspensky was trapped. All ways out of Essentuki were cut off. For a man who had been taught that human beings are in prison, caged by the walls of "sleep," the less metaphorical restraints of a bandit Bolshevik regime, complete with robberies, executions, requisitions, and famine were, one suspects, a gold mine of opportunities to remember himself. And indeed it was during this period that Ouspensky discovered a strange new self-confidence. Not ordinary self-confidence, but rather a "confidence in the unimportance and the insignificance of the self, that self which we usually know." If something big faced him, something that would strain his every nerve, this new "I," he believed, would be equal to it. And this, Ouspensky wrote, was the result of his work with Gurdjieff.

By early January 1920, Ouspenky found himself in Constantinople, washed to the edge of Europe by the great wave of the revolution. Friends had died; he and his family had suffered hardship, although they were, he tells us, more fortunate than others. But in a city already brimming over with refugees, expositors of esoteric psychologies were not in the best position to earn a living. Once again challenged by necessity, Ouspensky supported his family by teaching English—which he spoke poorly—to his fellow Russian émigrés.

He managed to get other work as well. He set up lectures and started groups, discussing psychology and philosophy in relation to esotericism. Gurdjieff soon arrived, and the two worked together in what now seems like a last honeymoon of fruitful activity before the categorical split.

Although Ouspensky still had his doubts, he agreed to help Gurdjieff translate material for his ballet, *The Struggle of the Magicians*, perhaps a more apt swan song for their collaboration than either suspected at the time. They visited the Mevlevi dervishes in Pera, the European quarter of the city, where Gurdjieff had begun one of his many Institutes for the Harmonious Development of Man. They also walked through the maze of bazaars, where, more than likely, Gurdjieff wangled a deal or two on the side.

And then the miracle happened. If Ouspensky had hoped to find the miraculous through Gurdjieff, what happened to him in June 1921 was an event almost specifically designed to make him believe in the possibility of fairy godmothers. Unknown to Ouspensky, Claude Bragdon, an artist and publisher, had put out a translation of Ouspensky's first major work, *Tertium Organum* (1912), in America. To his amazement, Bragdon discovered he had a bestseller on his hands. A young Russia émigré, Nicholas Bessaraboff, had arrived at Bragdon's door with a copy of Ouspenky's metaphysical prose poem on time, eternity, and the fourth dimension, demanding Bragdon publish it. Bragdon, who spoke Russian, read it and did publish it. Now, through the offices of the *New Age*, he had managed to track its mysterious author down and sent him a substantial royalty check. Ouspensky must have had a peak experience when it arrived. He had made contact with the outside world at last. It had come to him.

Ouspensky asked Bragdon for help getting himself and his family to London. Difficulties arose. Then the second miracle occurred. Bragdon received a telegram from Viscountess Rothermere, wife of a powerful English newspaper baron. *Tertium Organum* had stimulated her immensely, and she absolutely had to meet its publisher. An afternoon visit to Bragdon's office led to another telegram, this one to Ouspenky: "DEEPLY IMPRESSED BY YOUR BOOK TERTIUM ORGANUM WISH TO MEET YOU NEW YORK OR LONDON WILL PAY ALL EXPENSES."

And if that wasn't miracle enough, a cable for one hundred pounds was included, a sizeable sum at the time. Visas were all that remained, difficult things to come by for refugees. But again luck was on Ouspensky's side. J. G. Bennett, who would later become the third major interpreter of Gurdjieff's work (after Ouspensky and Orage), was at that time an agent in the British Foreign Service, stationed in Constantinople. He had met Ouspensky and had helped him secure a place for his meetings. Bennett arranged the paperwork, and Ouspensky was soon on his way to London.

Previously a hungry philosopher, lifting suitcases for his daily crust, the forty-three-year-old Ouspensky arrived in London as the feted author of a bestselling work on metaphysics, a romantic survivor of the collapse of Russia, the teacher of a system that was a revolution in its own right, and the darling, at least for a time, of a wealthy and beautiful woman eager to introduce him to London's literary circles and wine and dine him at her expense. Surely Ouspensky had found the miraculous.

His arrival in London was greeted with the kind of reception every author fantasizes about at least once in his lifetime. Colin Wilson, no stranger to a sudden eruption into fame, gives an idea of what Ouspensky found when he got off the boat in August 1921. It was, he writes, a "fairy-tale reception" by the "beautiful Lady Rothermere":

> Then a magnificent party . . . at which they ate with gold knives and forks from what looked like gold plates. The fairy-tale continued. When Ouspensky gave his first lectures in Lady Rothermere's studio in St. John's Wood, they were attended by the cream of London's intelligentsia, including Orage, T. S. Eliot, Aldous Huxley, Gerald Heard. . . . Ouspensky's buildup had been impressive: a mysterious foreign philosopher who had been forced to flee from the Bolsheviks, had endured immense hardships and . . . against all the odds, had made his way to London . . . his lectures turned out to be . . . startlingly new and strange. The conquest was complete. Ouspensky had become the intellectual flavor of the month.

Ouspensky's first stop was a hotel in Bloomsbury, that part of London associated with the British Museum, Virginia Woolf, and Lytton Strachey. Later he moved to a small studio flat in Gwendwr Road, near Baron's Court, paid for by Lady Rothermere. The building, now demolished, was described by Kenneth Walker as one of Victorian style, "uniformly dismal in pattern." During a meeting with Ouspensky, Walker inspected the atmosphere of the philosopher's "cell," Ouspensky's home for more than a decade. He found a small bed, two armchairs, a gas fire, a low bookcase, and a low mahogany table. Books, papers, letters, pens, a typewriter, a camera, a galvanometer, and an "unknown scientific instrument" wrestled for space. Reproductions of the old masters hung on the walls. A hunk of bread and a half-eaten tin of sardines atop the mantelpiece suggested "a nice disregard for the inconvenience of which life is chiefly composed."

Soon Ouspensky began to hold meetings to expound Gurdjieff's system, first in Lady Rothermere's studio, later in Warwick Gardens in Kensington. Eventually, as attendance at his lectures grew in the 1930s, Ouspensky acquired first a large house in Gadsden, Kent, then Lyne Place in Virginia Water, a suburb of London. In Lyne Place he set up an institute comparable in size, character, and ambition to Gurdjieff's own Prieuré in Fontainebleau, outside Paris.

Although Ouspensky had doubts about his teacher and was resolved to scale the uncongenial heights of higher consciousness on his own, he nevertheless continued to have faith in the system. Gurdjieff himself may have gone off the rails—readers can consult the evidence and conclude for themselves—but the "work" was Ouspensky's bedrock. At least until his bizarre last meetings in 1947, shortly before his death. In the end, after teaching the system for more than twenty-five years, a sick, tired, and searingly honest Ouspensky shocked his audience in Colet Gardens by announcing that there was no system and that they had to start again from the beginning and think for themselves.

Before Gurdjieff, Ouspensky was an enthusiastic artist-philosopher, in love with nature, beauty, art, and the fairer sex and confident of our ability to push the mind into the farther reaches of reality. And after Gurdjieff? What is evident is that the years of fruitless search, his demanding work with Gurdjieff, and the challenges of living in a war-torn and revolutionary Russia took their toll. J. G. Bennett tells the story that males in the Ouspensky clan alternated between life-loving Peters and world-denying Demians. Ouspenksy was dealt an uncomfortably equal share of both characters. Few in London knew the Ouspensky who had caroused with Russian Symbolist poets at the Stray Dog Café, headquarters of prerevolutionary St. Petersburg's avant-garde. But if any had, they would have noticed a change. The Ouspensky who arrived in a London eager for spiritual renewal and soon to give forth a *Waste Land* offered a teaching that would shock many, disgust a few, and exhilarate others. He was a very serious man. Peter hadn't disappeared entirely; Ouspensky was fond of good food and frequented a Chinese restaurant on Oxford Street. But Demian had gained the upper hand.

And the teaching? Man is "asleep." We are robots driven by outside forces. We think we have will and consciousness and that we are free, but this belief is precisely the prison that cages us and the soporific that keeps us asleep. The first move in our "war against sleep" is to realize our absolute mechanicalness and inability to *do*.

Many were not taken with the message, or with the messenger. The occultist A. E. Waite, author of books on mysticism and Kabbalah, is said to have walked out of one of Ouspensky's lectures, saying, "Mr. Ouspensky, there is no love in your system." Dry, professorial, and brief, Ouspensky was unlike the effervescently charming Orage, who believed that in Ouspensky he had found "someone who knows"—until, that is, he met Gurdjieff himself. Unflatteringly compared in appearance to Woodrow Wilson, the stout, solid, close-cropped, white-haired, pince-nezed Ouspensky lacked Gurdjieff's incomparable panache.

The writer Rom Landau, author of the bestselling *God Is My Adventure* (1939) and later a student of Ouspensky, tells of Ouspensky's reserve, born of a "self-discipline not to indulge in superfluous little activities. . . . Whatever Ouspensky had to say was said in the shortest possible way, and was followed by silence." Some described him as a man of "dominant, if not domineering type of character." Others said he looked like "a dejected bird, huddled up in a rain storm."

In many ways, Ouspensky was not really cut out for the role he began to play in England and later in the United States: that of the esoteric teacher. He was, first and foremost, a romantic philosopher and writer. The admirably hard-edged logic and unswerving precision he brought to the "work" was in many ways paid for by the slow desiccation of his more gentle artistic side. This side became known to people who got close to him, like C. S. Nott, whose *Journey through This World* (1969) gives an account of meeting Ouspensky at Lyne Place in 1936. By then the recourse to drink that would eventually kill him had begun, as had the nostalgic evocations of older times in Russia.

But before these sad developments, Ouspensky enjoyed an opportunity to influence a select audience of London's literary lights that any thinker, esoteric or otherwise, would envy. One can imagine the exchange, verbal or perhaps more subtle, between him and T. S. Eliot as they eyed each other at Lady Rothermere's soirée. Much of Eliot's poetry deals with the themes of time, eternity, and our inveterate tendency to avoid seeing the world as it really is, all themes central to Ouspensky's message. In *Four Quartets* Eliot wrote, "Time present and time past / Are both perhaps present in time future / And time future contained in time past," an Ouspenskian proposition if there ever was one.

Ouspensky made some significant immediate conquests among the intelligent men and women who attended his lectures, dissatisfied with the spiritual lassitude of England between the wars. Along with acquiring Kenneth Walker, a Harley Street physician and author of a spiritual autobiography, Ouspensky also stole one of C. G. Jung's early followers in England, in whom Jung had high hopes. Maurice Nicoll, later to be the author of *Psychological Commentaries on the Teachings of Gurdjieff and Ouspensky*, returned from his first encounter with Ouspensky so excited that he shook his pregnant wife awake to tell her of the experience. Before meeting Ouspensky, during a dark night of the soul, Nicoll had prayed to the god Hermes for a message, a way out of confusion. Ouspensky, he believed, was his answer, and he later went on to teach the system in his own heavily Christianized variant.

This descent is familiar to students of the Fourth Way. What is less known is Ouspensky's influence on literary history. Like *Tertium Organum's* effect on the Russian avant-garde, the presence of Ouspenskian ideas in English literature between the wars is a topic rarely discussed in the academy. But along with Eliot, ideas from the system appeared in the work of other major writers. The character of Mr. Proptor in Aldous Huxley's *After Many a Summer* (1939) is said to be modeled on Ouspensky. "All personality is a prison," Huxley's character says. "Potential good is anything that helps you get out of prison"—an aphorism that wouldn't be out of place in one of Ouspensky's lectures. In *The Harmonious Circle: The Lives and Work of G. I. Gurdjieff, P. D. Ouspensky, and Their Followers* (1980), James Webb suggests that Huxley researched the perennial philosophy by attending Ouspensky's meetings and points out that Huxley refers to "negative emotions," a central "work" term, in his description of a bad trip in *The Doors of Perception* (1954). Charles Williams, the Dante scholar and member of the latter-day Hermetic Order of the Golden Dawn, wrote a novel dealing with aspects of time and space familiar to Ouspensky. *Many Dimensions* (1931) posits a universe very much like Ouspensky's new model. But not all were well-disposed to Ouspensky's theories. The vitriolic artist and writer Wyndham Lewis, who characterized Gurdjieff as a "Levantine psychic shark," lumped Ouspensky together with other "fancy time theorists" like Henri Bergson, Marcel Proust, and Charlie Chaplin in his critique of modern culture, *Time and Western Man* (1927).

Yet it was as a philosopher of time, and not as an exponent of Gurdjieff's system, that Ouspensky would have his most direct influence on English letters. September 22, 1937, was the first night of the famous playwright and novelist J. B. Priestley's new play, *I Have Been Here*

Before. Visitors to the Royal Theatre that evening read in their programs that the strange theories of time and recurrence of the character of Dr. Gortler were based on an "astonishing book," *A New Model of the Universe,* by one P. D. Ouspensky. As Kenneth Walker's account tells us, Ouspensky, suffering a hangover from his uncertain days in Russia, conducted his teaching in an atmosphere of secrecy, shunning public attention. To have his name read each night by the audience of a West End theater while watching a hit play must have seemed quite a cosmic joke, although it certainly didn't hurt the sales of the book. Priestley, having been exposed to Ouspensky's ideas about eternal recurrence and six-dimensional time, dove deeply into them, but never managed to meet the man himself. His very celebrity made Ouspensky see him as a potential "threat to security." This didn't stop Priestley, a "time-haunted man," from spending the rest of his career in some ways pursuing the questions raised by Ouspensky and later by Maurice Nicoll.

The symbiosis between art and reality is rife with irony. The very atmosphere of mystery that surrounded Ouspensky, made public through Priestley's play, lent him the dramatic air of the character of Dr. Gortler and, for a time, attracted more attention to him. Foreign, enigmatic, preoccupied, impatient of the civilities that make up our usual social conduct, Ouspensky appeared in the consciousness of cultured London in the late 1930s much like Priestley's character. A man from elsewhere and elsewhen, refugee or exile, who in some strange way saw deeper into the ambiguous face of the world than the rest of us. A man for whom time, indeed, was of the essence. If Ouspensky's later years were filled with sadness and disappointment, his journey out of the chaos of his homeland into a literary London eager to hear his message has the aura of myth. It is a timeless symbol of the eternal search that the Ouspensky of *Tertium Organum* believed was the meaning of life.

Jean Gebser:
Leaping into the Unknown

The German-born cultural philosopher Jean Gebser (1905–1973) is one of the most important thinkers of the twentieth century. Unfortunately, only some of his work has been translated into English. This is a loss. Gebser's ideas about the "structures of consciousness" and his belief that we are experiencing the rise of a new form of consciousness, which he called the "integral," offer some of the most fruitful insights into understanding the state of Western consciousness in the first decade of the twenty-first century.

Although writers and thinkers like Ken Wilber, William Irwin Thompson, Georg Feuerstein, Colin Wilson, and Daniel Pinchbeck have discussed Gebser's ideas in different ways (I write about him at length in *A Secret History of Consciousness*), Gebser's name rings few bells among average readers. This isn't surprising. Gebser comes out of the Central European intellectual tradition, the stream of Western thought that produced such important but difficult philosophers as Georg Wilhelm Friedrich Hegel, Martin Heidegger, and Jürgen Habermas—intensely stimulating thinkers all, but not noted for easy reading. Also, Gebser's untimely death at the age of sixty-eight meant that for the most part his influence was limited to his immediate circle. If a few readers of this essay are inspired by it to tackle Gebser for themselves, I'll consider its purpose fulfilled.

Those inspired readers will certainly face a demanding challenge. Gebser's magnum opus, *The Ever-Present Origin* (first published in

Germany in 1949 but not translated into English until 1984) is an immense, six-hundred-page-long exploration into an insight—a "lightning-like inspiration," as he called it—that first came to Gebser in Spain in 1931. This insight, that a new kind of consciousness was beginning to appear in the West, came to Gebser through his study of poetry, particularly that of the Austrian poet Rainer Maria Rilke. As he unraveled his insight, Gebser soon saw that evidence for this new consciousness could be found in developments in science, too. In fact, the more he thought about it, the more Gebser discovered signs of this new consciousness in practically all aspects of Western culture. For the next eighteen years, Gebser gathered and organized his thoughts on what he called an impending "mutation" in consciousness, the most immediate manifestation of which was what he called the breakdown of the "mental-rational structure" of consciousness, the dominant scientistic, rationalististic, reductive paradigm that has held sway over the West for the last few centuries. In 1949, when the first part of *The Ever-Present Origin* appeared—to be followed by the second in 1952—Gebser marshaled some of the most convincing arguments that a shift in Western consciousness was indeed taking place and that its consequences would be felt by people of his and the following generations. In other words, by us.

Gebser was born in Posen, in what was then Prussia, in a particularly pivotal year. In 1905 Albert Einstein formulated his special theory of relativity, and it was Einstein's work, along with that of other thinkers and writers, that provided Gebser with powerful evidence for the peculiar shift in our "time sense" that characterizes the new structure of consciousness he saw unfolding. A few years earlier, in 1900, Sigmund Freud had published his groundbreaking *Interpretation of Dreams*. Other seminal developments occurred around the same time. The physicist Max Planck completed his theory of the quantum, which led to the overthrow of classical physics, and the philosopher Edmund Husserl established the foundations of phenomenology, the rigorous investigation of consciousness that would lead to existentialism. For a thinker whose work would focus on sudden shifts in the history of consciousness, Gebser certainly picked an auspicious year in which to be born.

By the time he was ten, all of Europe had exploded into the First World War, and Gebser's childhood was filled with chaos and disruption. Early on he had an experience which helped him deal with a world thrown into confusion. While at preparatory school, he jumped from a high dive into a deep pool. He felt that the leap into the pool was also a leap into the unknown, and it was then that he lost his "fear in the face of uncertainty." "A sense of confidence began to mature within me," he wrote, "a confidence in the sources of our strength and being and in their immediate accessibility." Gebser christened this confidence *Urvertrauen*, "primal trust," a change from the *Urangst*, or "primal fear," that characterizes much of our experience of life.

Gebser's "primal trust" helped him negotiate many future leaps into the unknown. One occurred when he abandoned an apprenticeship at a bank for an uncertain career in literature. In his early twenties, with a friend Gebser started a literary journal and publishing company. Many of his first poems saw print then, and throughout his life Gebser continued to write poetry, finding in language a way into the mysteries of consciousness; it was also around this time that he discovered Rilke. The economic collapse of the Weimar Republic devastated Gebser's family and provided yet another confrontation with uncertainty; they lost their savings and were brought to ruin, and Gebser himself felt the effect of the growing strength of Hitler's National Socialism at first hand. It was Rilke's vision of a state of being in which one could affirm everything—the "praise in spite of " embodied in the Angel of the *Duino Elegies*—that helped Gebser through this time, and he finally overcame the thoughts of suicide that oppressed him. Yet by 1929, the campaign of political violence unleashed by Hitler's Brown Shirts convinced Gebser it was time to make another leap.

For the next few years Gebser lived as a kind of European internal exile, moving about from Italy, back to Germany, then to Paris, then southern France, finally settling in Spain in 1931. It was here, as noted, that his original inspiration into the structures of consciousness occurred, yet Spain too was only a temporary haven. These were the years when Generalissimo Francisco Franco's fascists overthrew the legitimate socialist government, and in 1936, Gebser barely missed being killed when he left Spain for France just hours before his Madrid apartment was shelled. As it was, he was almost executed at the border. In Paris he moved among the artistic elite and became friends with many of them, including Pablo Picasso. But Paris was no home either. In August 1939 Gebser crossed from France into Switzerland two hours before the borders were closed; not long after, the Nazis marched below the Arc de Triomphe.

As it did for so many others, Switzerland proved a safe haven for Gebser, and it was here that he settled down to his life's work. For the next thirty-three years, Gebser devoted his life to unpacking his ideas about the changes taking place in Western consciousness, lecturing, among other places, at the Institute of Applied Psychology in Zürich. Here he met and befriended C. G. Jung, with whose work his own has much in common; this led to Gebser lecturing at the C. G. Jung Institute and also to his becoming a familiar contributor to the annual Eranos Lectures held in Ascona, Switzerland, where his name became associated with other thinkers like Mircea Eliade, Gershom Scholem, Erich Neumann, Henry Corbin, and Jung himself, who presided over the gatherings. After World War II Gebser traveled, visiting India, the Near East, and North and South America. Although his work is, for the most part, focused on the cultural and collective expressions of the current "mutation" in consciousness, in Sarnath, India he had a mystical experience that moved him deeply. His "satori experience," as he called it, was so profound that he was reluctant to speak of it; he kept it a secret until 1971, when he revealed it to his biographer and interpreter, Georg Feuerstein. He wrote to Feuerstein that it was a "transfiguration and irradiation of the indescribable, unearthly, transparent 'Light.'" It was, he said, a "spiritual clarity, a quiet jubilation, a knowledge of invulnerability, a primal trust," linking this new affirmation of life with his first, youthful leap into the unknown. After it, he felt "recast inwardly," adding, "Since Sarnath, everything is in its proper place."

Like his early experience, the insight at Sarnath helped Gebser to deal with his growing ill health, a demanding workload, and the recognition that the West had moved again into a dangerous time of uncertainty. The Cold War was heating up, and Gebser was convinced that "the crisis we are experiencing today . . . is not just a European crisis." It was "a crisis of the world and mankind such as has occurred previously only during pivotal junctures." In 1966 Gebser's health collapsed; asthma, which had troubled him throughout his life, worsened, and he was forced to curtail his travels and abandon new projects. Gebser never fully recovered, but he continued to write, and he was aware of the new interest in consciousness and spirituality that had arisen in the Mystic Decade of the '60s and early '70s. Speaking to a younger generation of readers eager to know more about different forms of consciousness and familiar with the work of Sri Aurobindo and Pierre Teilhard de Chardin (two other thinkers concerned with the evolution of consciousness), in a preface to a new edition of *The Ever-Present Origin*, Gebser wrote that "the principal subject of the book, proceeding from man's altered relationship to time, is the new consciousness, and to this those of the younger generation are keenly attuned." By the time Gebser wrote this, in 1973, ideas of a new consciousness had spread throughout the counterculture, and the attempt to launch a new paradigm—known variously as the Aquarian Age, the New Age, the Aquarian Conspiracy, and other titles—had taken root. Gebser died the same year, convinced that a new kind of consciousness was being born. It would be a difficult labor, however, and there was no guarantee against miscarriage.

What is the new consciousness Gebser saw on the rise? Here it is impossible to give more than a brief indication of what he spelled out in meticulous and fascinating detail in *The Ever-Present Origin*, and readers wanting a good introduction to his work should find a copy of Georg Feuerstein's excellent *Structures of Consciousness*

CHAPTER FOURTEEN

(Integral Publishing, 1987) or my own *Secret History of Consciousness*. Gebser believed that consciousness has gone through four previous "structures," each achieving a further separation and distinction from an atemporal, immaterial, spiritual source that he called "origin." This is not a simple, temporal beginning, but an eternal "presence," an "ever-present reality" that is by nature "divine and spiritual," "before all time," and "the entirety of the very beginning." For readers who are already scratching their heads, I should point out that one of the difficulties in reading Gebser is that he unavoidably uses language based on our present consciousness structure to speak about types of consciousness that precede or transcend it. With this in mind, a comparison of Gebser's "origin" with the "implicate order" of the physicist David Bohm may be helpful. Bohm's implicate order is also an atemporal unity out of which our present universe of space-time emerges, and the process of this emergence is rather like those Japanese paper pellets that, when dropped into water, unfold into various shapes. For Gebser the "pellet"—"origin"—contains within itself, in a form of "latency," the further consciousness structures that unfold over time. "Latency" is a central idea in Gebser, embodying the "demonstrable presence of the future."

The first consciousness structure to unfold is the *archaic*. In essence, it isn't appreciably different from origin. It is, Gebser says, "zero-dimensional," being little more than the first slight ripple of difference between origin and its latent unfolding. Here consciousness is identical with the world; it's a state of "complete non-differentiation between man and the universe." Out of this the *magical* structure unfolds. This doesn't differ greatly from the archaic, but the separation from origin has increased. Where in the archaic structure there is *identity* between consciousness and the world, in the magical structure there is *unity* between them. At this stage, our ancestors lived in a kind of group or tribal consciousness, which was still strongly linked to nature. Gebser speaks of a "vegetative intertwining of all living things" during this stage, and he aptly links Jung's notion of synchronicity—and the effects of "magic"— to this structure. Gebser makes it clear that all of the previous consciousness structures are still present in consciousness today, and that the magical structure is at work in all experiences of group consciousness. Sadly, for Gebser, the most immediate expressions of group consciousness were the Nazi rallies that drove him out of Germany. Today, many people who believe they are entering "higher" states of consciousness by receding back into a "tribal" mode are actually simply sinking into a uncritical acceptance of the magical structure.

Out of the magical comes the *mythic*. Here consciousness achieves a further differentiation; it is characterized by *polarity*. Here for the first time appear yin and yang, earth and sky, male and female, space and time, and the other binary oppositions that constitute our experience. Here the "soul," an interior, "inner space" in contrast to an external one, appears. Gebser associates this structure with the Greek myth of Narcissus, the youth who fell in love with his own reflection. The soul first sees itself reflected in the outer world in this structure, and the dominant mode of experience here is feeling, which is expressed through the ancient myths. Thought, as we understand it, had yet to appear.

This happens in the *mental-rational* structure, the next to arrive. Undoubtedly by now readers are wondering exactly *when* these different "structures" appeared. Admittedly, Gebser is less than clear about dates. For the mental-rational structure's earliest appearance he suggests 1225 BC; the previous structures, the archaic and magical, reach far back, into our distant, pre–*Homo sapiens* beginnings, and the mythic to around the time the earliest civilizations arose after the last Ice Age. While, as noted, all previous consciousness structures remain active, if obscured, in our present consciousness, the mental-rational structure is the one we are the most familiar with, given it is our own. In this structure, thinking as we understand it begins. Here the separation and differentiation from origin is complete. Consciousness—the ego—is on its own, and this condition is expressed, among other ways, in an increase in violence and a loss of community. Here, for the first time, the notion of time in a linear sense arrives. For the archaic and the magical, there is no time as we know it but only a kind of intermittent "now," with long stretches of unconsciousness in between. For the mythic, there is the cyclical time we associate with the eternal round of the seasons and the perpetual circling of the stars. With the mental-rational structure, "straight-line" time appears, and with it a profound awareness of death. Needless to say, it is out of the mental-rational structure, and its ability to narrow its attention and focus on details rather than participate in the whole—as the archaic, magical, and mythic structures do to different degrees— that science, with all its achievements and problems, arises.

Gebser argues that prior to the emergence of a new structure, the previous structure enters a "deficient" mode, characterized by its breakdown; what had previously been a "credit" and an advantage now becomes a "deficit" and a handicap. Gebser believed that the mental-rational structure entered its "deficient" mode in AD 1336 with the rise of perspective, the switch from the "two-dimensional," "embedded" vision of the world common in the Middle Ages (think of tapestry) to the acute awareness of distance and space embodied in the paintings of the early Renaissance (think of landscape paintings). Here, he believes, consciousness achieved its complete "liberation" from origin.

The deficient mode of the mental-rational structure reached its most radical form in the nineteenth century, with the triumph of the rationalist-reductive paradigm mentioned earlier, and Gebser believed that throughout the twentieth century it was in the process of deconstructing itself. The clearest evidence for this, Gebser argued—aside from all the global problems we have inherited—was a profound change in our sense of time. As mentioned, he points to Einstein's relativity as one example, but there are many more, taken from art, literature, philosophy, music, and other cultural forms. On a more mundane level, however, I can offer one example, unknown to Gebser, in which time as we knew it has been abolished. Anyone who uses Tivo or podcasts is no longer bound by the idea of a certain television program or radio broadcast being on at a "certain time." The whole Internet experience, in fact, has altered our way of thinking about both time and space. There is the constant "flow" of information, and nowadays people "connect" over vast distances instantaneously; we have more "contact" with people on the other side of the planet than we do with our actual neighbors. On a less innocuous note, the many crises affecting us today—ecological, social, economic, political—can all be traced to the effects of the mental-rational structure of consciousness entering its deficient mode.

This breakdown, Gebser believed, was a kind of clearing away, a making space for the new consciousness structure, the "integral," to arrive. As its name suggests, in this structure, the previous four structures are integrated. The integral structure is characterized by what Gebser calls an "aperspectival" awareness, a transcending of the "perspectival" in the same way that the perspectival was a transcending of the "pre-perspectival." In the integral structure, origin becomes perceivable, the spiritual "concretized," and the "uncreated light" manifest. Gebser's Sarnath insight, in which he experienced satori, is an example of what he means by the integral structure of consciousness. As with all shifts from one structure to another, the transition is by no means guaranteed, and the experience, both individual and collective, is traumatic. Recent developments in the world economy, brought about by the short-sighted greed for immediate gain associated with the deficient mental-rational mode, would have only convinced Gebser that he was right.

This brief summary is light-years away from doing Gebser's ideas justice, and I can only hope that it motivates some readers to seek him out for themselves. He is difficult, but then so is anything of value. To my mind, *The Ever-Present Origin* presents the most convincing evidence that, at the present time, the West—the entire planet, in fact—is facing a perilous leap into the unknown. It also suggests ways in which we can make that leap, as Gebser did, with primal trust.

CHAPTER FIFTEEN

Owen Barfield and the Evolution of Consciousness

O wen Barfield is not a name on everyone's lips. Even in the relatively small community of scholars who should know him, mention of Barfield usually brings looks of ignorance or, at best, dim recognition. "Oh yes. He's that fellow who was friends with C. S. Lewis, wasn't he?" Given some familiarity with Barfield's work, you might receive a more in-depth but not necessarily more enlightened remark, as I did when mentioning him to a university academic in a London pub. "Barfield?" he said. "You mean that Coleridge loony?" With perceptions like this, is it surprising that a writer of books about the origin of language and the evolution of consciousness should be unknown to the general public? Hardly. But when that writer is one of the most interesting thinkers of the twentieth century, one can only comment, "More's the pity."

Owen Barfield—scholar, philosopher, novelist, friend of C. S. Lewis, and interpreter of Rudolf Steiner—was indeed one of the most remarkable men of the twentieth century. Born in North London in 1898, Barfield fought in the First World War, lived through the Blitz, endured the tensions of the Cold War, and at the end of his life was concerned with the increasing balkanization of the globe. In terms of intellectual and cultural history, his career was a chronology of twentieth-century thought. Early books, like *History in English Words* (1926) and *Poetic Diction* (1927), were written in the suffocating atmosphere of logical positivism, when philosophy as a "love of wisdom" was abandoned for a sterile hairsplitting of syntax. Barfield's belief in language as an archaeological record of the evolution of consciousness, and as a means of metalogical insights, was as at odds with the reigning zeitgeist as you could get.

Both books were praised by the critics, but it wasn't Barfield's destiny to make a living as a writer. A contributor to *The New Statesman, The London Mercury,* and T. S. Eliot's *Criterion,* Barfield was nevertheless forced by financial pressures to enter his family's law firm and dropped out of the literary scene in the early '30s, only occasionally publishing articles in philosophical journals. Nearly thirty years later he made an impressive comeback with *Saving the Appearances* (1957), subtitled "A Study in Idolatry." In this book Barfield wondered how disciplines that took physics as their model could reject its most revolutionary insights—for instance, that the observer is inextricably linked to the observed—as biology did when it claimed that consciousness emerged from blind matter, and as behavioral psychology did when it went one further and declared there was no such thing as consciousness at all. Barfield, taking physics at its word and drawing on the epistemological theories of Coleridge and Goethe—with a large helping of Rudolf Steiner—went in the opposite direction, toward a "participatory universe," in which human consciousness, far from being a ghost in the machine, is master of ceremonies.

More books followed, as did stints in various American universities as visiting lecturer. *Worlds Apart* (1963), a heady Platonic dialogue, took the fragmentation of modern thought as its theme. In *Unancestral Voice* (1965), Barfield's fictional alter ego, Burgeon, discovers a superintelligent entity, the Meggid, residing in his unconscious mind. Through a series of conversations, the Meggid introduces Burgeon/Barfield to the system of thought with which Barfield, in those circles in which he is known, is associated: Rudolf Steiner's Anthroposophy. In these works, as in the books that followed—*Speaker's Meaning* (1967); *What Coleridge Thought* (1972); *The Rediscovery of Meaning* (1977); *History, Guilt, and Habit* (1979); and also in his collection of Anthroposophical essays, *Romanticism Comes of Age* (1944)—Barfield argues for the supremacy of imagination as both a creative agent and a pathway to knowledge: an idea that would become his trademark.

So when in 1996, shortly before his death, I had an opportunity to visit Barfield and talk with him about his life and work, I jumped at the chance. It's not every day one gets to spend an afternoon with a walking history of twentieth-century thought.

As anyone who has read his books knows, the focal point of all of Barfield's work was the evolution of consciousness. Not ashamed to admit that he was what Isaiah Berlin would call a "hedgehog"—one of those who, unlike the fox, know only one big thing—Barfield admitted that all his books were about the same thing. He said as much during my visit to the Walhatch, the residency estate in Forest Row, East Sussex, where Barfield lived at the end of his life. Comparing his work to that of his friend C. S. Lewis, Barfield remarked: "There's an early Lewis and a later Lewis; that's why he's interesting to scholars. They can mark the stages of his development. There's none of that with me. I never developed. As an accurate but perhaps unkind critic remarked, I've been saying the same thing for fifty years. The only difference now is that it's seventy years, not fifty."

But repetition isn't always a drawback—especially when what you say is as interesting as what Barfield said. During the hour or so I spent with him, we talked about his life and work, Rudolf Steiner, the challenges facing a spiritual life in the modern age, and what he saw coming at the end of the twentieth century. Though supremely lucid, witty, and in good health, it wasn't surprising that Barfield tired easily; a casual chat seemed more appropriate than a rigorous interview. Sitting in a massive armchair, white-haired, thin, and clutching a smoldering pipe, a sagacious, bespectacled Barfield seemed happy to receive a visitor, especially one eager to discuss ideas. What follows is a brief introduction to Barfield's philosophy, sprinkled with some comments he made during my visit.

The basic idea behind the evolution of consciousness is, as Barfield briefly put it in *Romanticism Comes of Age,* "the concept of man's self-consciousness as a process in time." Compare this with the notion of the "history of ideas." In the standard history, an ancient Greek and a postmodern American have very different ideas about the world, but both perceive the world the same way—with the understanding that our ideas, informed by modern science, are closer to the truth. There's no difference between the consciousness of the ancient Greek and ours, only between the concepts "inside" it. When we open our eyes, we see that same world. It's just that we have better ideas about it.

For Barfield this is totally wrong. Not only do their ideas about the world differ, but the world the ancient Greek saw and the one we see are not the same. The kind of consciousness we enjoy—if that's the right word for it—is very different from that of an ancient Greek, a Greek of late antiquity, a person from the Middle Ages, or even one of the early modern age. Not only our ideas about things, Barfield tells us, but our consciousness itself has evolved over time. And if we are to take seriously the contention of philosophers like Immanuel Kant—that the world we perceive is a product of our perceptual apparatus—then a world produced by a different consciousness at a different time will be, well, different.

One of the most fascinating conclusions Barfield draws from this is that all ideas about the prehistoric world, from paleontological textbooks to popular depictions like *Jurassic Park,* are, at the least, questionable. "They project a picture of that world as it would be seen by a consciousness alive today. We have no way of knowing what that world looked like to a different consciousness because we have no record from a consciousness of that time. We can only speculate." To the contention that we have the paleontological record, Barfield replies, "It's nevertheless our consciousness that discovers fossils and organizes them into the schemata of ancient life."

But if we can only speculate about the nature of reality before the rise of consciousness, there is another record, one we find not by digging through ancient earth, but by scrutinizing ancient texts. This is language, the study of which, according to Barfield, is "a kind of archaeology of consciousness." As he writes in *History in English Words*: "In language . . . the past history of mankind is spread out in an imperishable map, just as the history of the mineral earth lies embedded in the layers of its outer crust. But there is this difference: whereas the former can only give us a knowledge of outward, dead things . . . language has preserved for us the inner, living history of man's soul. It reveals the evolution of consciousness."

And whereas the orthodox view of evolution has a preexisting, external world much like our own, made up of distinct, independent, impermeable objects, the record left us by language, Barfield argues, suggests something different.

"The standard understanding of the evolution of language," Barfield told me, "is that all words referring to something spiritual or abstract have their origin in literal meaning." So when we refer to a "spirit" enlivening the physical body, what we are talking about is something like breath. We find this is in the Hebrew *ruach* and the Greek *pneuma*. Or, as he wrote in *Poetic Diction*: "It is a commonplace . . . that, whatever word we hit on, if we trace its meaning far enough back, we find it apparently expressive of some tangible, or at all events, perceptible object or some physical activity. . . . Throughout the recorded history of language the movement of meaning has been from the concrete to the abstract."

The result of this is the insight, voiced by thinkers like Emerson and Nietzsche, that modern language, with its abstract terms and nuances of meaning, is, as Barfield writes, "apparently nothing . . . but an unconscionable tissue of dead, or petrified, metaphors." The further we dig into language, the more metaphors we find.

But there is something wrong with this, Barfield says. Etymologists, like the famous oriental scholar Max Müller, believed that early humans began with very simple, literal words and phrases for tangible, perceptible things. Then, with the "dawn of reason" (itself a metaphor), our ancestors began to use these phrases metaphorically, to describe inner and outer experience. If we take this theory to its logical conclusion, Barfield argues, "the result should be that today, after millennia of metaphor building, we should all be spouting poetry whenever we speak." And likewise, we should, being so much more sophisticated, find poetry from earlier times rather less poetic. Neither of which, of course, is true. Homer still thrills like nothing else. Müller and his followers erred, Barfield believes, by adopting an unquestioned Darwinian approach to the history of language. Just as simple organisms became more complex over time, so too language evolved, they believed, from simple "root" words denoting tangible "things" into our highly abstract and metaphorical speech. "The only problem with this is the evidence from language itself," Barfield argues.

What the history of language tells us, Barfield says, is that "our ancestors didn't use language as Müller believed, because they did not see the same world. Müller projected the world as perceived by late-nineteenth-century European man into the past. That's why the only account of the history of language he could give was one that followed Darwinian ideas of progress." The kind of world that ancient man saw—and that our ancestors continued to see until recent times—was, Barfield believes, one in which human consciousness "participated." At that stage of the evolution of consciousness, the distinction between "self" and "the world" was not as rigid as it is today. What Müller misunderstood as metaphoric was early man's ability to see the "inside" of things, just as we now are aware of our "inside"—our minds. Accounts of nature spirits; folktales and myths about fairies, nymphs, and sylphs; legends of gods walking the earth are all rooted in this "participatory consciousness." This was the kind of world (and consciousness) that poets like Blake, Coleridge, and Goethe believed in and at times felt. It was also the kind of consciousness described by Rudolf Steiner. Barfield calls it "original participation."

"Original participation," according to Barfield, is a "primal unity of mind and nature, with no separation between inner and outer worlds." At that point, nature, he believes, was as subjective, as inward as we are. But what happened is that gradually "unconscious nature" became localized in human consciousness. If we think of unconscious nature as a vast ocean, and the initial separation of human consciousness as wavelets lifting themselves up from the surface, we'll have an idea of what Barfield means. Gradually this process continues, with an increasingly tenuous link between our new "self"-consciousness and its "unconscious" source, until we arrive at our present state: a completely other "outside world" with separate islands of inwardness housed within our individual skulls. At this point we are as far away from original participation as we can get.

But although some bemoan our exodus from the garden, this estrangement from our source was absolutely necessary, Barfield tells us. The path of evolution, he says, isn't a straight line; it is much more like a U. The left hand of the U traces the path from original participation to our current estrangement from nature. In the nineteenth century, with the rise of a completely materialistic explanation of the world, including the most immaterial thing we know, consciousness, we reached the bottom of the U. Now we are just beginning to make our ascent back up, this time on the right hand of the U. This is the essential difference. Because now we can begin to "participate" in the world not passively—as we had as primitive humans and as animals do today—but actively, by becoming conscious of the power of our imagination in creating "the world." (And if we need an example of the difference between active and passive participation, we need merely recognize the difference between our dreams, over which we have little or no control, and the consciousness of an artist or poet focused intently on his work.) We had to leave the security of original participation in order for consciousness to take the next step in its evolution. Having hit bottom on the evolutionary curve, we are beginning our ascent to what he calls "final participation," a conscious participation in the cosmos.

The idea of an evolution of consciousness, though unorthodox, is not as strange today as it may have seemed when Barfield first presented it. Since then it's been argued by several thinkers, notably Jean Gebser in *The Ever-Present Origin* and the Jungian theorist Erich Neumann in *The Origin and History of Consciousness*. But Barfield's take on it is peculiar, and perhaps his most startling idea is a reversal of the standard materialist account of mind's emergence from matter. Rather than being a fluke product of evolution, consciousness itself, Barfield argues, is responsible for "the world."

That's why there is no answer to questions about the origin of language when asked from the conventional view. Asking about the origin of language, Barfield says, is like asking about the "origin of origin." Language didn't come about as a way to imitate, master, or explain nature, as it is usually assumed, because "nature" as we understand it didn't exist until language did. According to Barfield, the polarities of mind/world and language/nature are the result of splitting up original participation. To understand language, Barfield tells us, we must imagine ourselves back to a stage at which human consciousness hadn't yet separated from its unconscious background. At that point there was no "nature" and no "consciousness"—at least not as we understand it. "Nature," Barfield tells us, didn't exist until human consciousness came into its own. The "world" as we see it is the result of millions of years of work by the human mind.

The fact that we are unaware of our participation in the world accounts for our alienation from nature, as well as our mastery of it. The "idols" of the subtitle to *Saving the Appearances* are the "collective representations"—the phenomena of the physical world—as they are understood by modern science; that is, as completely unrelated to the imagination. Modern science, developing during consciousness's "flight from nature," in Steiner's phrase, is "idolatry" because it's forgotten the source of the phenomena it studies. Indeed, in behavioral psychology, linguistic philosophy, and various other materialistic disciplines, idolatry goes so far as to deny the very existence of that source. Having shaped a fascinating, complex, and seemingly infinite world, consciousness loses itself in it, a situation described in Hindu and Buddhist teachings as "falling into *maya*," or illusion. But while Hindu and Buddhist thought advise an escape from maya, Barfield, working in the Romantic tradition, proposes a less austere strategy. If the phenomenal world is shaped by some part of the mind of which we are not conscious, then to avoid "idolatry" we need to become conscious of that power. As he writes in *Saving the Appearances*, "If appearances are correlative to human consciousness and if human consciousness evolves, then the future of the appearances, that is, of nature herself, must indeed depend on the direction which that evolution takes."

To slightly alter a hackneyed phrase, the fate of the world isn't in our hands but in our minds.

When Barfield wrote *Saving the Appearances*, several developments threatened to steer the evolution of consciousness in an undesirable direction. Logical positivism and linguistic philosophy had emptied language of meaning. Science, with its increasing fragmentation of nature and itself into smaller and smaller parts, could offer no vision of wholeness. Nearly half a century later, not much has changed. To think of our "postmodern condition" and to read Barfield is chilling. The "accelerating increase in that pigeon-holed knowledge of more and more about less and less" which "can only lead mankind to a sort of idiocy . . . with the result that there will in the end be no means of communication between one intelligence and another" will sound ominously accurate to anyone familiar with today's universities. But science and philosophy are not the only things that bode ill for the future of nature. The arts too are implicated. "Imagination," Barfield says, "is not simply synonymous with good." Given the accelerated pace of evolution, he warns that without some moral guidance, unrestrained imagination can let loose a riot of fantasy and obsession, not all of a wholesome character. Given our ability to "morph" reality or to "virtually" create it, the wedding of imagination and technology can result in something like *Star Trek's* holodeck, which our hunger for raw sensation and aesthetic shock will use to fashion environments like those in *Naked Lunch*. If that is the case, then Barfield's warning of our moving into a "fantastically hideous world" may prove uncomfortably timely.

Talking of the Internet, Barfield remarked wearily that "something that is supposed to bring people together seems to be doing quite the opposite," creating self-enclosed fantasy worlds where people "indulge in sexual eccentricities without ever meeting another human being." At ninety-seven, you might excuse him for not being quite with it, but little of import passes Barfield by. From hackney cabs to space shuttles, he's seen it and had something to say about it. So I asked him the inevitable: what did he think was in store for us as we approached the millennium? "Well," he said, plunging a match into his Holmesian pipe, "I'm an optimist in the long run, but a pessimist in the short. The ecological situation is really quite bad. And society is more fragmented than ever; even with this 'information age' we never hear the end of it. I'd like to think we'll avoid a catastrophe, but I don't know. . . . But I'm certain we're moving into a new stage of consciousness, as Steiner said. People are beginning to feel a sense of unity. What we need is time for this to spread, for more people to become aware of it."

Sitting in Barfield's living room, looking at the rows of books by his friends—Eliot, Charles Williams, Tolkien, and, of course Lewis—I was glad for once to be in the presence of a flesh-and-blood wise old man and not only a psychic archetype. Meeting the person behind ideas you have been excited by for years gives a sense of the living past that is the essence of tradition. It also makes one feel the importance of keeping that past alive. Having closed out a century saturated in materialism and hooked on a culture of violence and nihilism, we need Owen Barfields more than ever before.

Chapter Sixteen

The Strange Death of James Webb

O n the afternoon of May 8, 1980, after two years of a deep, paralyzing depression and at least one psychotic episode, the brilliant Scots historian of the occult James Webb put the barrel of his shotgun to his head and blew his brains out. He was thirty-four. In the 1970s Webb had made a name for him with his fascinating if skeptical histories of occultism, *The Occult Underground* (1974) and *The Occult Establishment* (1976). In 1980, *The Harmonious Circle*, Webb's study of G. I. Gurdjieff, P. D. Ouspensky, and their followers had just been published, and Webb's career was looking good. He was a regular contributor to *Encounter* and also to the encyclopedia *Man, Myth, and Magic*, and his performance at Trinity College, Cambridge, had been so stellar that a biennial James Webb Memorial Prize is awarded there in his honor.

Webb's books combine a painstaking research into the occult and an ironic dismissal of it, the kind of know-it-all rationalism we might expect from a Cambridge graduate. But at the time of his suicide, Webb had changed his mind about the kinds of experiences he had chalked up to delusion, fantasy, and a post-Enlightenment craving for the irrational. In his last days, Webb was convinced that the nervous breakdown that cast him into suicidal madness had also revealed dimensions of reality that could only be called supernatural. He found himself "catapulted into a larger universe" filled with altered states of consciousness and profound visions of "cyclical time."

The experience was not all revelation. Webb also showed the classic signs of paranoid schizophrenia. His publisher, he claimed, was persecuting him. Worse still, he was convinced that a certain group of French Freemasons had it in for him. Such remarks suggest Webb's change of heart about the supernatural was nothing more than the pathetic result of his tragic breakdown. Yet the circumstances surrounding his death were unusual and raise the suspicion that the dividing line between madness and occult revelation may not be as clear cut as we suppose.

How and when Webb's madness began are unclear; even as a schoolboy at Harrow he was considered brilliant but perhaps a little unstable. After his death, his widow—even more skeptical of the supernatural than he—refused to discuss the matter, preferring, understandably, to forget the tragic business. By most accounts Mary Webb was a no-nonsense, practical woman who loved her husband but had little insight into his brilliance and even less into his obsessions, and it is a fair guess that she may have felt that his interest in the occult was somehow responsible for his madness. That Webb married a woman with little of his intellectual spirit and less sensitivity to his experiences is one of the strange things about the affair. It does account, however, for his relationship with another woman, Joyce Collin-Smith. Many an unsympathetic wife has driven her husband into other arms, but in Webb's case the attraction of the other woman wasn't sexual but psychic.

Webb first encountered Joyce Collin-Smith in 1972. At the National Liberal Club in London, she gave a lecture to the Astrological Association on the life and work of her brother-in-law, Rodney Collin. Webb was interested in Rodney Collin because, as one of the main followers of Ouspensky, Collin would feature prominently in Webb's book on Gurdjieff. Webb had come to the lecture intending to ask Joyce for an interview about her brother-in-law.

By the time she met Webb, Joyce Collin-Smith had run the gamut of spiritual teachers. In the 1950s she practiced the Gurdjieff "work" with Rodney Collin at his commune in the suburbs of Mexico City. Before this she had been involved with Dr. Frank Buchman, founder of Moral Rearmament. She was also a follower of Pak Subuh, the Indonesian mystic and founder of the Subud movement, which included J. G. Bennett among fellow "work" members. And, in the early days of the 1960s, she had been chauffeur and girl Friday to the Maharishi Mahesh Yogi before the Beatles discovered meditation and made the giggling guru a spiritual superstar. A former Fleet Street journalist, novelist, and officer in the Women's Auxiliary Air Force, Joyce was old enough to be Webb's mother; at the very least, she was an unusual candidate for spiritual adviser to a brainy twenty-six-year-old who found most of her pursuits pure hogwash.

And yet, at the very first meeting, Joyce knew Webb would play a large role in her life. She also knew he was fated for some strange destiny. As she recalled in her autobiography, *Call No Man Master* (1988), the minute she saw the tall, red-haired young man enter the auditorium, her "heart leapt." It was not love at first sight; on the contrary, in Webb she recognized a sinister, terrifying figure from a repeated nightmare of her childhood. In her dreams, a tall, red-haired young schoolmaster asked her to fetch something from a forbidding tower. Frightened at entering the tower alone, she nevertheless obeyed. Halfway up, in a desolate, empty room, the schoolmaster, raving mad, charged in and threw himself at her. She woke up each night, sweating and terrified. Now, more than forty years later, the mad schoolmaster had come to her lecture.

Joyce watched as he took a seat in the last row. She then gave her lecture, speaking, she recalls, almost solely to him. At the end of her talk, as she spoke with some of the audience, Joyce half expected the "schoolmaster" to erupt into maniacal laughter. But when the shy, diffident young man approached and explained that he was writing a book on Gurdjieff and wanted to speak with her about her brother-in-law, she was surprised at his gentle, almost apologetic manner.

They developed an immediate rapport. In Joyce's house in Sussex, they talked for hours about philosophy, religion, history, and her experiences with the occult. Precognitive dreams, visions, strange states of consciousness while practicing Transcendental Meditation and self-remembering, even communication with the dead. Webb was impressed. A brilliant scholar, his encounters with the occult had been strictly "armchair," but it's clear from Joyce's account that he was also attracted to something else.

Webb's family was well-off. Had he lived, Webb would have inherited a large estate at Blair Drummond, in Perthshire, Scotland. But relations with his family had soured over Mary. Class may have had something to do with it, but Webb's mother and stepfather were certain she wasn't right for him; when the couple did marry, it was against their wishes.

Estranged from his parents, finding little in common with Mary, Webb took refuge in his studies. His brilliance threw him far ahead of his contemporaries. Few could keep up with his discoveries; fewer still could speak intelligently about them. And now he had met someone who seemed to know all about the occult from the inside, someone who also took an immediate liking to him and gave him encouragement and approval. Joyce quickly became a kind of surrogate mother for Webb. He welcomed the ease and naturalness in her household, so different from the tension around his real parents. Later Joyce would claim that they had known each other in previous incarnations; this time they had met as a sort of mother and son.

Inevitably, Joyce compared their astrological charts; both were Capricorns with Leo rising. The points of contact among their stars suggested to Joyce that James could indeed have been her son—had she had one—and the association with the mad schoolmaster faded from her consciousness. Their rapport deepened; her affection for the young scholar grew. More and more, Joyce was reminded of her relationship with Rodney Collin, who, as we shall see, also died in mysterious circumstances. As their philosophical conversations continued, they began to experience a kind of telepathy; each knew the other's thoughts before a word was spoken. Their rapid exchange developed into a kind of verbal shorthand. Repeatedly, Joyce felt a curious sensation of déjà vu. At one point, during tea on a summer afternoon, Webb asked Joyce for "another piece of cherry cake." Immediately Joyce was reminded of another childhood dream, this one involving a Tibetan background, a fantasized "brother," and cherries. Increasingly she felt that they were indeed "two beings who had incarnated within reach of each other many times in different roles."

Several months later Joyce's husband's ill health forced her to sell their Sussex house, and they moved to a cottage in the New Forest. Money was scarce; she had to take what work she could find, mostly lecturing and doing horoscopes. Not long after, she got a call from "Jamie," as she called Webb. He wanted to double-check some material for the Gurdjieff book. He and Mary had married recently and had just returned from a honeymoon in the Orient. Joyce was glad to hear from him, but thought he sounded strange, "rather low and glum," unlike his usual cheerful self. Webb wanted to visit her, but Joyce put him off; her husband's health would make things difficult. But she promised to ring him soon about lunching with him in London.

Something in Webb's call made Joyce check his chart again. She saw the familiar qualities, "fiery, vigorous, and tenacious," so much like her own. But there was something else. Webb's stars indicated a depressive tendency, an inclination to withdraw deeper into himself as he got older. She didn't know it at the time, but Webb had just done that. He had amassed an incredible library and spent more and more time alone, immersed in his research. Friends and literary acquaintances saw less and less of him. His marriage, too, seemed shaky. Webb worked well into the night, often falling asleep at his desk, amidst volumes of Jacob Boehme, Raymond Lully, and other occult philosophers. What had been an admirable dedication to work now seemed a full-fledged obsession. Joyce warned Jamie of the dangers but, like any good Faust, he ignored them.

The next time they spoke, Joyce felt certain something had happened. It was then that Webb told her of being persecuted by his publishers and raved about the French Freemasons. He was ill with flu, and Joyce urged him to relax. But Webb's mental deterioration had begun. He didn't ring again and, to her later regret, Joyce's own affairs prevented her from telephoning him. The next time she heard from him, Webb had already plunged into madness.

"My life has just emerged from a nightmare," Webb wrote some time later. "I had a full-scale nervous breakdown, with hallucinations, visions, and a fine repertoire of subjectively supernatural experiences. Hoist with my own petard, some would say." The cool rationalism that called occultism a "flight from reason" seemed helpless before the kinds of experiences he had gone through. "Despite the undoubtedly hallucinatory nature of many of my experiences," he wrote, "a residue remains which I simply have to take seriously." He tried to fit what was happening to him into some system, calling on Gnostic notions of Aeons and Hindu *kalpas*. But the visions were too vivid and extraordinary to be neatly filed into some metaphysic. The gist of them had to do with time. The world had become a kind of Heraclitean flux. He had seen "molecules."

Webb's letter was postmarked Durisdeer in Dumfrieshire. He and Mary had left London and had moved into a renovated old church. Joyce wrote back immediately. Webb replied at great length; he thought she had rebuffed him in his hour of need. His account of his breakdown was harrowing. He had been in and out of various hospitals, had been in the hands of several psychiatrists, was doped on Largactil (sold in the United States as Thorazine) and had only just escaped electroshock therapy. He had given up writing and was just barely keeping his sanity. Joyce berated herself for not responding sooner. She soon made up for this. During the next five months she and Webb exchanged a lengthy and extraordinary correspondence. Two or three times a week several pages of Webb's increasingly wild account reached her door.

He wrote of a "shattering vision of the wheel of life." He saw his previous incarnations. He became convinced that there is a "principle of consciousness which is not merely the result of a congeries of experience"—what Ouspensky had called the *linga sharira*, the "long body" that extends through countless lives. But the worst was that there seemed to be no stability. Things would not "stand still." No sooner did he look at something than he saw its entire history, its present, past, and future. An oak was an acorn, then a rotting mass of mulch. Although he believed there was a way out, Webb shrank from the knowledge that we are all "imprisoned in the coils of cyclical time."

Finally Joyce could offer something more than sympathy. She was familiar with these visions. During her time with the Maharishi, she had experienced the same phenomena, the result of too much Transcendental Meditation. It had brought her to the brink of suicide. She suggested exercises to keep his mind focused in time. These helped for a while, but increasingly Webb's thoughts turned to death. He wrote to Joyce that "Rodney Collin was quite right about the importance of dying properly." He also said that he had "revised my opinion about the manner of Ouspensky's death."

Strange deaths were indeed not uncommon among professors of Gurdjieff's "work." When Gurdjieff died in 1949, the doctor performing the autopsy declared that his internal organs were in such bad condition that he should have been dead years before; Gurdjieff had apparently willed himself to stay alive. Ouspensky's death was even stranger. He was obsessed with time; his particular fascination was eternal recurrence, the notion that, with slight variations, our lives repeat, over and over. The only possibility of escape is in becoming more conscious. In his last days, a sick and dying Ouspensky visited various favorite sites, fixing them in his mind, in order to remember them in his next recurrence. Weird psychic phenomena occurred; in his efforts to die consciously, witnesses report that Ouspensky had become telepathic.

And when, on October 2, 1947, Ouspensky passed away, Rodney Collin, his closest disciple, locked himself in the room next to his master's and did not emerge until a week later. He told his wife—and Joyce—that he had been in communication with Ouspensky the entire time. Nearly ten years later, on May 3, 1956, Collin himself would die after falling from a tower in Cusco, Peru. He was found in a position resembling the crucified Christ; earlier he had prayed that a crippled peasant boy be cured, and he had told his wife that he had offered God his body in exchange. There is some suspicion that he too had attempted to "die consciously." Webb had written skeptically about the events around Ouspensky's and Collin's death. Now he had reason to change his mind.

Joyce considered the possibility that Jamie was going through some kind of self-inflicted initiatory process. She knew that their conversations had opened him to the reality of the occult. His armor of skeptical rationality had cracked; in his letters he spoke of curious precognitive dreams and of a kind of Gnostic personal myth. He had long fantasized that he was a member of a crew whose spaceship had crashed on an alien planet. Enslaved by the natives, they soon forgot their past. But occasionally a dim memory stirred, the crew members recognized each other, and they recalled their mission. "The tragedy," he told her, "is infinitely far distant, the adventure infinitely long. And we are ageless, ageless."

Had Webb been allowed to explore these intuitions, it's possible he may have survived. But after several months of having him around the house, Mary forced him to take a job. They didn't need the money. Understandably, she felt that some work might give her husband some ballast. But she really had no insight into his plight and little patience for his talk about the soul, later telling Joyce that she considered all that sort of thing "rubbish." A copywriting job for an Edinburgh advertising agency was not quite what Webb needed. The uncongenial atmosphere had the opposite effect, throwing him deeper into alienation. His letters to Joyce became wilder. He was researching a book about esoteric movements in Scotland but he "couldn't get the pattern of it anymore." More and more, he believed, someone was after him because he knew too much,

Finally, Joyce decided she had to see him. By this time their telepathic link had increased. She had visions of him at his desk and could feel a pain in the back of his neck, a vulnerable spot he shared with both her and Rodney Collin. She could hear him crying at night and in her mind reached out to comfort him. Although she had never been there, she had images of the grounds around the house; later, after Webb's death, she saw that these had been accurate. In a few weeks, she and her husband would go to Scotland for their holiday. She decided then to see Jamie.

It was too late. On the afternoon before their trip, Joyce heard Webb's voice calling her name. "I'm coming," she answered mentally. Then something like an enormous explosion went off in her head. At once she told her husband, "Something is wrong with Jamie." He said it was her imagination. Incredibly, she didn't telephone. When they arrived at their holiday cottage there was a message to ring Mary. At three o'clock the previous day, Webb had shot himself. Joyce later discovered the immediate cause was a domestic quarrel.

Visiting Webb's parents, Joyce discovered the full extent of his madness. One night, he crouched before the fire at their estate, repeating the Lord's Prayer over and over and muttering repeatedly, "What is it all about?" On another occasion, he ran out into the night in a state of hysteria. He waded waist-deep across a river to reach Dunblane Cathedral twelve miles away, where he banged furiously on the door. Oblivious to those around him, for a few weeks the "mad schoolmaster" was certifiably insane.

Inevitably, Joyce blamed herself for not seeing him sooner. Jamie had plunged into a dark night of the soul, and she hadn't been there for him. Her sense of guilt, then, may account for what followed. She began to feel Webb's presence. First he asked her to visit his mother. Then he wanted her to carry on his work. Two visits to a medium convinced her that some part of Jamie had survived. Material emerged unknown to her that later proved unsettlingly accurate. The voice told her that he "would come to her," asking that she get his books from Mary, who "doesn't understand them." "Make a replica of me," it said.

At first Joyce was thankful for these messages. But then she felt that something was "not right" about them. This was not the "whole" Jamie, merely bits and pieces of him. Jamie, or some part of him, didn't know he was dead and wouldn't "move on." Joyce began to feel that she was being "taken over." Eventually, a clergyman friend of spiritualist persuasion offered to say a requiem to help Webb relinquish his attachment to the world. Satisfied that the rite would not interfere with them finding each other in the next incarnation, Joyce agreed. As she and the clergyman read the prayers in the candle-lit chapel, she felt something lift up from her consciousness and take flight. Jamie had moved on.

There was one other curious phenomenon. During her first wave of grief, Joyce found herself crying aloud, "Why didn't you help him?" In the depths of her anguish she heard a voice that said, "I did." At the same time she saw a face, dark-haired, dark-eyed, with a deep, penetrating gaze. She thought it might have been Rudolf Steiner. At the time of his suicide, Webb had been commissioned to write a book about Steiner, a task that later went to Colin Wilson. Wilson remarked that if Webb's earlier books were anything to go by, his book on Steiner would surely have been skeptical. Considering Webb's strange and tragic death, had he survived, I wonder if Wilson would have been right.

Sources

Colin Wilson and Faculty X

Wilson, Colin. *Access to Inner Worlds*. London: Rider, 1983.

_____. *Beyond the Occult*. New York: Ballantine, 1987.

_____. *Frankenstein's Castle: The Right Brain, Door to Consciousness*. Sevenoaks, UK: Ashgrove Press, 1980.

_____. *Mysteries*. New York: G. P. Putnam's Sons, 1978.

_____. *The Occult*. New York: Random House, 1971.

Discovering Swedenborg

Larsen, Robin, ed. *Swedenborg: A Continuing Vision*. New York: Swedenborg Foundation, 1981.

Schuchard, Marsha Keith. "The Secret Masonic History of Blake's Swedenborg Society." *Blake, An Illustrated Quarterly* 26, no. 2 (Fall 1992).

_____. "Swedenborg, Jacobites, and Freemasonry." In Erland J. Brock et al., eds., *Swedenborg and His Influence* (Bryn Athyn, PA: Academy of the New Church, 1988).

_____. *Why Mrs. Blake Cried: William Blake and the Sexual Basis of Spiritual Vision*. London: Century, 2006.

_____. "Yeats and the Unknown Superiors: Swedenborg, Falk, and Cagliostro." *The Hermetic Journal* 37 (Autumn 1987).

Staley, Michael, ed. *Emanuel Swedenborg: Essential Readings*. Berkeley: North Atlantic, 2003.

Jan Potocki and the Saragossa Manuscript

Potocki, Jan. *The Manuscript Found in Saragossa*. Translated by Ian Maclean. London: Penguin, 1996.

Arkon, Daraul. *Secret Societies: A History*. New York: MFK, 1989.

Éliphas Lévi: The Professor of Transcendental Magic

Lévi, Éliphas. *Transcendental Magic*. Translated by A. E. Waite. London: Rider, 1984.

McIntosh, Christopher. *Éliphas Lévi and the French Occult Revival*. London: Rider, 1971.

The Alchemy of August Strindberg

Strindberg, August. *Inferno / From an Occult Diary*. Translated by Mary Sandbach. Harmondsworth, UK: Penguin, 1979.

The Inimitable Madame B.

Blavatsky, Helena Petrovna. *Isis Unveiled*. Pasadena, CA: Theosophical Publishing House, 1972.

_____. *The Secret Doctrine*. Edited by Michael Gomes. New York: Tarcher Penguin, 2009.

Cranston, Sylvia. *HPB: The Extraordinary Life and Influence of Helena Petrovna Blavatsky*. New York: Tarcher Putnam, 1993.

Washington, Peter. *Madame Blavatsky's Baboon*. London: Secker & Warburg, 1993.

Rudolf Steiner: The Dweller on the Threshold

Belyi, Andrei, Aasya Tugenieff, and Margarita Voloschin, eds. *Reminiscences of Rudolf Steiner*. New York: Adonis, 1987.

Steiner, Rudolf. *Autobiography*. Translated by Rita Stebbing. New York: Rudolf Steiner Publications, 1977.

Manly Palmer Hall: The Secret Teacher

Hall, Manly P. *The Secret Teachings of All Ages*. New York: Tarcher Penguin, 2003.

Jenkins, Philip. *Mystics and Messiahs: Cults and New Religions in American History.* Oxford: Oxford University Press, 2000.

Sahagun, Louis. *Master of the Mysteries: The Life of Manly P. Hall.* Port Townsend, WA: Process Media, 2008.

Dion Fortune: Psychic Warrior

Chapman, Janine. *Quest for Dion Fortune.* York Beach, ME: Samuel Weiser, 1993.

Fortune, Dion. *Applied Magic.* York Beach, ME: Samuel Weiser, 2000.

_____. *Psychic Self-Defense,* http://jacquesricher.com/occult/psychic. pdf; accessed Feb. 21, 2014.

_____. *The Secrets of Dr. Taverner.* http://www.golden-dawn.com/eu/ UserFiles/en/File/pdf/taverner.pdf; accessed Feb. 21, 2014.

_____. *What Is Occultism?* York Beach, ME: Samuel Weiser, 2001.

Richardson, Alan. *Priestess: The Life and Magic of Dion Fortune.* Wellingborough, UK: Aquarian, 1987.

Aleister Crowley: The Beast Himself

Crowley, Aleister. *The Confessions of Aleister Crowley.* New York: Ballantine, 1971.

_____. *The Diary of a Drug Fiend.* New York: Samuel Weiser, 1970.

Symonds, John. *The Great Beast.* St. Albans, UK: Mayflower, 1973.

Julius Evola: Mussolini's Mystic

Drake, Richard. "The Revolutionary Mystique and Terrorism in Contemporary Italy." In Peter Merkel, ed., *Political Violence and Terror.* Berkeley: University of California Press, 1986.

Evola, Julius. *Revolt against the Modern World.* Rochester, VT: Inner Traditions, 1995.

Godwin, Joscelyn. *Arktos: The Polar Myth in Science, Symbolism, and Nazi Survival.* Kempton, IL: Adventures Unlimited, 1996.

Jung and the Occult

Bair, Deirdre. *Jung: A Biography.* New York: Little, Brown, 2004.

Brome, Vincent. *Jung: Man and Myth*. London: Scientific Book Club, 1979.

Jung, Carl Gustav. *Memories, Dreams, Reflections*. London: Fontana, 1989.

_____. *The Red Book: Liber Novus*. New York: W. W. Norton, 2009.

Wehr, Gerhard. *Jung: A Biography*. Translated by David M. Weeks. Boulder, CO: Shambhala, 1987.

Ouspensky in London

Ouspensky, P. D. *In Search of the Miraculous*. New York: Harcourt Brace, 1949.

Webb, James. *The Harmonious Circle: The Lives and Work of G. I. Gurdjieff, P. D. Ouspensky, and Their Followers*. New York: G. P. Putnam, 1980.

Jean Gebser: Leaping into the Unknown

Feuerstein, Georg. *Structures of Consciousness*. Lower Lake, CA: Integral Press, 1987.

Gebser, Jean. *The Ever-Present Origin*. Ohio: Ohio University Press, 1984.

Owen Barfield and the Evolution of Consciousness

Barfield, Owen. *History in English Words*. West Stockbridge, MA: Inner Traditions/Lindisfarne, 1985.

_____. *Poetic Diction*. Hanover, NH: Wesleyan University Press, 1987.

_____. *Saving the Appearances*. New York: Harcourt, Brace & World, n.d.

The Strange Death of James Webb

Collin-Smith, Joyce. *Call No Man Master*. Bath, UK: Gateway, 1988.

Webb, James. *The Occult Establishment*. La Salle, IL: Open Court, 1976.

Wilson, Colin. "James Webb and the Occult." *Light* 1, no. 2 (Summer 1982).

Index

INDEX

INDEX

Quest Books

encourages open-minded inquiry into
world religions, philosophy, science, and the arts
in order to understand the wisdom of the ages,
respect the unity of all life, and help people explore
individual spiritual self-transformation.

Its publications are generously supported by
The Kern Foundation,
a trust committed to Theosophical education.

Quest Books is the imprint of
the Theosophical Publishing House,
a division of the Theosophical Society in America.
For information about programs, literature,
on-line study, membership benefits, and international centers,
see www.theosophical.org
or call 800-669-1571 or (outside the U.S.) 630-668-1571.

Related Quest titles

The Esoteric World of Madame Blavatsky,
by Daniel Caldwell

The Gnostic Jung and the Seven Sermons to the Dead,
by Stephan A. Hoeller

In Search of P. D. Ouspensky,
by Gary Lachman

Pauli and Jung: The Meeting of Two Great Minds,
by David Lindorff

To order books or a complete Quest catalog,
call 800-669-9425 or (outside the U.S.) 630-665-0130.

About the Author

G ary Lachman is the author of several books on the link between consciousness, culture, and the Western esoteric tradition. He writes for numerous publications in the United States and United Kingdom and lectures frequently on his work in the US, the UK, and Europe. His books have been translated into a dozen languages, and he has appeared in numerous documentaries. A founding member of the rock group Blondie, as Gary Valentine he was inducted into the Rock and Roll Hall of Fame in 2006. Born in New Jersey, since 1996 he has lived in London. Visit his website at garylachman.co.uk.